Arthur Schopenhauer

Titles in the series Critical Lives present the work of leading cultural figures of the modern period. Each book explores the life of the artist, writer, philosopher or architect in question and relates it to their major works.

Arthur Schopenhauer

Peter B. Lewis

REAKTION BOOKS

11/24/12
#16.95

Dedicated to Dorothy, Emma and Megan

Published by Reaktion Books Ltd
33 Great Sutton Street
London EC1V ODX, UK

www.reaktionbooks.co.uk

First published 2012

Printed and bound in Great Britain
by Bell & Bain, Glasgow

British Library Cataloguing in Publication Data
Lewis, Peter B.
Arthur Schopenhauer. – (Critical lives)
    1. Schopenhauer, Arthur, 1788–1860.
    2. Philosophers – Germany – Biography.
    I. Title II. Series
    193–DC23

ISBN 978 1 78023 021 4

Contents

Abbreviations

BM	*On the Basis of Morality*, trans. E.F.J. Payne (Indianapolis, IN, 1977)
EFR	*Schopenhauer's Early Fourfold Root*, trans. F. White (Aldershot, 1997)
FR	*The Fourfold Root of the Principle of Sufficient Reason*, trans. E.F.J. Payne (LaSalle, IL, 1974)
FW	*On the Freedom of the Will*, trans. Konstantin Kolenda (Indianapolis, IN, 1960)
G	*Gespräche*, ed. Arthur Hübscher (Stuttgart, 1971)
GB	*Gesammelte Briefe*, ed. Arthur Hübscher (Bonn, 1978)
MR I–IV	*Manuscript Remains*, ed. Arthur Hübscher, trans. E.F.J. Payne (Oxford, 1988), vols I–IV
PP I–II	*Parerga und Paralipomena*, trans. E.F.J. Payne (Oxford, 1974), vols I–II
TFP	*The Two Fundamental Problems of Ethics*, trans. Christopher Janaway (Cambridge, 2009)
VC	*On Vision and Colors*, trans. E.F.J. Payne (Oxford, 1994)
WN	*On the Will in Nature*, trans. E.F.J. Payne (Oxford, 1992)
WWR I–II	*The World as Will and Representation*, trans. E.F.J. Payne (New York, 1969), vols I–II

Arthur Schopenhauer in Frankfurt am Main, March 1859.

Introduction

Arthur Schopenhauer was possessed by a genius for philosophy that determined the course of his life, though he did not become aware of this gift until he was in his early twenties. A similar pattern was displayed a century later in the career of Ludwig Wittgenstein. Yet whereas Wittgenstein's philosophical genius was quickly and enthusiastically acknowledged by the most eminent intellectuals of his day, Schopenhauer had to wait for recognition until his 66th year. Throughout the 35 years of neglect he endured between the publication of his masterpiece, *The World as Will and Representation,* and his rise to fame, Schopenhauer never doubted that his voice would be heard. For, he believed, he had produced a philosophy for the world, a philosophy that would benefit mankind by providing the solution to the riddle of existence. Schopenhauer lived just seven years to enjoy his renown. But for 50 or more years after his death, his ideas were celebrated by leading intellectuals, writers and artists, and his name became a byword for philosophical greatness. 'I might have been a Schopenhauer or a Dostoyevsky!', cried Uncle Vanya in 1897.[1]

Schopenhauer's name no longer has that cachet, the title of fashionable philosopher having transferred to twentieth-century figures such as Heidegger, Sartre or Wittgenstein. Yet, securely established as one of the great philosophers, he has the paradoxical reputation of being both the supreme philosopher of pessimism and one of the few philosophers whose work is a pleasure to read. His lucidity, directness and wit make his ideas, especially in the late essays, more accessible than the turgid labourings of other nineteenth-century German philosophers. And, though there is in his work no shortage of technical discussion of interest to specialists, Schopenhauer's primary concern is always to address the great questions of philosophy: the meaning and value of life, the nature of art and of morality. There is no more eloquent portrayal, outside of the Old Testament, of the misery and vanity – the pointlessness – of life than Schopenhauer's.

Regarding himself as a missionary of truth to the human race (MR IV, p. 487), Schopenhauer devoted his life to his genius. His greatest fear was that circumstances, whether poverty, war or marriage, would prevent him from continuing his philosophical work. He led a solitary existence, within the limits imposed by his private income, and maintained a distance from his family and his friends. In addition to his naturally gloomy temperament he was embittered by the persistent neglect of his achievement, so was apt to behave intemperately in his relations with other people. To consider the life of such a man independently of his work would, as Simone Weil understood, inevitably result in emphasizing his shortcomings as a human being. Schopenhauer put the best of himself into his philosophical work. Hence his biography should look at his life in relation to his thought. The failings of his life are not glossed over but recognized 'as limitations rather than as essential elements of his genius'.[2]

Curiously, given the enthusiasm of the British for Schopenhauer, the first comprehensive biography in English did not appear until 2010. David E. Cartwright's detailed study rightly pays tribute to the many pioneering works in German, of which the most significant recent intellectual biographies have been those by Rüdiger Safranski and the late Arnold Hübscher, the doyen of Schopenhauer scholars.[3] While this biography is heavily indebted to all three, its inspiration is the compact volume published in 1890 by William Wallace, then Whyte's Professor of Moral Philosophy at the University of Oxford.[4] It appeared in a series of modestly priced critical biographies called 'Great Writers', which included poets, novelists and scientists as well as philosophers. Like the volumes of Reaktion's Critical Lives series, it was aimed at the educated general public.

Although Schopenhauer's works have long been available in a variety of English translations, the first volumes of a uniform scholarly edition appeared in 2009, an edition which will not be completed for some years.[5] The translations employed in this book are those by E.F.J. Payne (and, in the case of one essay, by K. Kolenda), which appeared in the 1950s and '60s, and are the translations most commonly relied upon by English students of Schopenhauer. The translations of the letters of Schopenhauer and his family, which are not available in English, are my own unless otherwise indicated.

What is life? A frenzy.
What is life? An illusion,
A shadow, a fiction,
And the greatest profit is small;
For all of life is a dream,
And dreams, are nothing but dreams.

Pedro Calderón de la Barcan, *La vida es sueño*, 1635

1

The Sins of the Father

Saturday, 20 April 1805, was the seminal day in Schopenhauer's life: the day his father was found dead in the canal behind their home in Hamburg. He had committed suicide. Arthur Schopenhauer was seventeen years of age and serving an apprenticeship with a local merchant in fulfilment of his father's plan that he should in due course take control of the family business. It was a plan Schopenhauer himself found increasingly difficult to reconcile with his yearning for a scholarly education. Within two years of his father's death, Schopenhauer took the first steps in an academic career that led to his emergence as a philosopher. Though he explicitly went against his father's wishes, Schopenhauer never ceased to pay tribute to his father's influence on his life, and never more fulsomely than in the unpublished dedication to the second edition of *The World as Will and Representation*:

> That I was able to develop and apply the powers, given to me by nature, to that for which they were destined; that I was able to follow my inborn impulse and to think and work for innumerable people, whereas no one did anything for me; for all this I thank you, my father, I thank your activity, your good sense, your thrift and thoughtfulness for the future. (*MR* III, pp. 414–15)

Schopenhauer's father, Heinrich Floris Schopenhauer, not only tried and failed to make him into a businessman, but tried and

failed to make him into an Englishman. In 1787, in the third year of
Heinrich's marriage to Johanna Trosiener, while on a leisurely tour
of Europe whose eventual destination was London, it was realized
that Johanna was pregnant. Heinrich was determined that his
hoped-for son should be born in England so that he would inherit all
the rights of citizenship beneficial to a merchant. Despite Johanna's
understandable anxiety about giving birth to her first child in a
foreign country without the support of her family, the couple settled
themselves comfortably in London in the late autumn of 1787.
But mortality rates in childbirth were high in the city, and it seems
that Heinrich's fears for the health of Johanna and her child eventually led them to decide at the end of November to undertake the
long and arduous journey home. The journey was not without its
dangers – their carriage was regularly bogged down and even over-
turned on the primitive tracks of Westphalia – and yet did not lack
pleasures: Johanna was especially taken with Düsseldorf and its
famous gallery of paintings. They returned to their home in Danzig
on New Year's Eve 1787 and, 'beloved and petted by mother, sisters
and relatives', Johanna 'became the happy mother of a fine hearty
boy' on 22 February 1788.[1] The child was baptised Arthur on 3 March;
the name was chosen by Heinrich because it appealed to his romantic anglophilia and because he believed it would be useful for a
businessman to have a name that remains unchanged in many
European languages.

Heinrich Floris Schopenhauer was born in the Free City of
Danzig (now Gdansk, Poland) in 1747 to a family of Dutch ancestry
with a long tradition as landowners, maritime merchants and
bankers. His education was acquired in the world of international
commerce. Living and working for many years in France and in
England inspired him with admiration for the civilization of both
nations, which were at that time far in advance, politically and
culturally, of the German-speaking countries. Heinrich became a
devotee of the works of Voltaire and was influenced by his enthusiasm

An anonymous watercolour miniature of Heinrich Floris Schopenhauer, the philosopher's father, 'circa his 40th year' according to Schopenhauer, therefore *c.* 1787.

for English civil liberties and literature, but it was Heinrich's seven-year domicile in London from 1773 that was the source of his anglophilia. As well as reading *The Times* every day – a habit he passed onto his son – he furnished his country home at Oliva, northwest of Danzig, in an English manner with English comforts, such as a well-stocked library and a garden laid out in the English style.[2] Heinrich's forceful personality found bodily expression in a short but muscular build and a large head with a wide mouth and prominent jaw, together conveying a powerful impression. More than a few of these attributes were inherited by his son: 'A pretty baboon he will be if he's like his father', was the comment of Heinrich's bookkeeper on hearing the news that his employer had a son.[3] Although Heinrich was spared the severe mental instability that afflicted his mother and two of his brothers, he seems to have inherited a disposition to depression, anxiety and shortness of temper. Arthur, too, was afflicted with this pathology, a legacy that tormented him throughout his life.

On his return to Danzig in 1780, Heinrich assumed control of the family business, and with his elder brother set up a new trading company that, in addition to their familiar roles as bankers and brokers, involved them in trading British manufactured goods for Baltic grain and raw materials. As the business flourished, Heinrich's resolute character, cosmopolitan spirit and business acumen gave him a status in Danzig society beyond that of a successful merchant. He was respected for his independent spirit as much as for his 'enlightened' views. At a time when Danzig was under threat from the antagonistic powers of Prussia, Russia and the Habsburg Empire, Heinrich was uncompromising in his loyalty to the city's traditional independence and civic freedoms. He had displayed the strength of his character and convictions when, on a visit to Berlin in 1773, he had proudly refused to move his business to Prussia despite the persistent courtship of Frederick the Great himself. And during the blockade of Danzig in 1783, when the Prussian general billeted on his father's estate at Ohra offered to permit the special importation of food for Heinrich's prized horses, Heinrich notified him of his thanks but also his determination to have the horses killed when the available feed was exhausted. This incident added to Heinrich's reputation among the city's hierarchy but was also to have near-disastrous consequences for him.

After almost 40 years as a bachelor, Heinrich proposed marriage to the eighteen-year-old Johanna Trosiener, also a native of Danzig

The young Johanna Schopenhauer, née Trosiener (1766–1838): novelist, salonnière, mother of the philosopher.

but one whose entire life had been sheltered within her family homes in and around the environs of the city. Like Heinrich, Johanna belonged to a family of the merchant class, though one less conspicuously successful than her suitor's. Her father was a political opponent of Heinrich's who, as a city councillor, attempted to persuade the citizens of Danzig to renounce their independence

Schopenhauer's birthplace in Gdansk, formerly Danzig.

and become subjects of the King of Prussia. Her mother's family, of Dutch extraction, included a great-grandfather who had been an ecclesiast in Holland.[4] The eldest of three daughters, Johanna was born in 1766. From her early years she had been befriended by Richard Jameson, the Scots minister to the British colony in Danzig. As the Trosieners' next-door neighbour he became Johanna's unofficial tutor, guide and counsellor. Under his benign influence she learned to speak English fluently and acquired a familiarity with the classics of English prose and poetry, her love of which she passed on to her son. With her youth, neat figure, brown hair and blue eyes, her charming manner and social skills, and her cosmopolitan outlook allied with her fascination for English culture and society, Johanna was evidently attractive to a crusty, unprepossessing bachelor such as Heinrich. Johanna frankly admitted in her memoirs that the relationship was not a love-match: for Heinrich marriage provided the opportunity to establish an heir for his business, while for Johanna it offered the brilliant prospect of her own home and with it everything that great wealth could buy.

Heinrich and Joanna were married on 16 May 1785. In the city they lived at Heiligengeist Strasse 117, where their son was born. In the summer months home was Heinrich's country estate at Oliva, though Heinrich spent the days of the working week in Danzig, returning only for weekends, usually with friends. Johanna lived a life of ease and luxury but also, for all but the winter months, of relative isolation, far from the busy streets and social life of the city. Unluckily for Johanna, Revd Jameson had been obliged to return to Scotland around the time of the marriage. It is easy to understand, then, her delight on learning early in the marriage that Heinrich proposed a grand European tour, ending in England. And he assured her that this was not a business trip, though he did intend to examine what domestic life was like in the land of liberty, as he called it.[5] Heinrich made clear to Johanna that changing political fortunes might compel him to move his business away from Danzig, and that England might be a suitable location for a new home. But on their return the very thought of uprooting seemed premature, as the familiar domestic routine re-established itself, with the joyful addition of a son. Moreover, Johanna's own family were soon to take up residence nearby when her father took a farm near Stutthof after the failure of his political manoeuvering obliged him to resign his seat on the Council and abandon his business. Johanna writes with manifest delight of the happy days she spent enjoying 'real country life' with her young son every year at the beginning of May.[6] Reflecting this carefree period, he maintained in later life that 'our years of childhood are a continuous poem' (*PP* I, p. 477). However, a portent of future troubles occurred in July 1789 when, for the first time ever during the working week, Heinrich visited Johanna in order to tell her the great news of the fall of the Bastille. The instability unleashed in Europe by the events of the French Revolution and its aftermath could not fail to impact upon the commercial activity of the merchant traders of Danzig. Still, it was almost four years before the blow fell. In March 1793, Prussia and Russia agreed the second partition of Poland, with Danzig to be annexed by Prussia. To make matters even worse for Heinrich, the commanding officer of the occupying army was none other than the Prussian general he had so resolutely rebuffed ten years earlier. Heinrich had little choice but to flee Danzig with his young family.

Heinrich chose to relocate his home and business to Hamburg. If London had been ruled out, then Hamburg was his most reasonable option. Hamburg was a sister Hanseatic city to Danzig and had similar, if not similarly robust, traditions of republican freedom. Like Danzig, Hamburg was a seaport and a flourishing centre of commerce with strong trading links to Britain and France. In fact, at this time Hamburg was enjoying an economic boom, having profited from the disruption to traditional continental trading networks caused by revolutionary politics in France. The city provided Heinrich with a good opportunity to re-establish his business after the losses consequent upon the hasty departure from Danzig. In just over three years the Schopenhauers were able to move from their rented accommodation in the Old City to a mansion at Neuer Wandrahm 92, where their neighbours comprised the elite of the city's merchants. Their new home, backing onto the canal, combined domestic and business functions, and its marble floors, ballroom, picture gallery and library were visible manifestations of the Schopenhauers' position at the forefront of Hamburg society.

In this environment Johanna flourished as never before. She made the most of the hectic social life of the city, entertaining in her grand home and attending other people's parties. For the first time since her marriage, Johanna found a social identity distinct from that of her husband. And she relished the role. With her charming manner and cheerful temperament, her fluency in numerous languages and her ability to relate easily to many different kinds of people, she became a successful socialite. Her success, though, came at the expense of discomfiting Heinrich and Arthur, whose more serious-minded disposition did not permit them to share Johanna's frivolous delights. Schopenhauer was in later years to speak of his mother's socializing with resentment. He complained that Johanna gave parties and amused herself while his father was sick and suffering bitter distress (G, p. 152). Nevertheless, Johanna's social accomplishments were to be of invaluable service to her in the years following her husband's death.

Among the Schopenhauers' acquaintances, and Johanna's guests, were ever-growing numbers of émigrés from revolutionary France. These included the Baron de Staël-Holstein, husband of the famous Madame de Staël, author and celebrated doyen of the Paris salons, a figure whom Johanna would later seek to emulate. The influence of the French added to the gaiety of Hamburg social life, which tended to be obsessed with practical commercial affairs. While Hamburg was not a significant cultural centre – the ageing poet Friedrich Gottlieb Klopstock was its sole luminary in this sphere – it was nonetheless a popular destination for European travellers, especially the English. There was a large and visible English presence in the city, which appealed to the anglophile Schopenhauers. Both William and Dorothy Wordsworth commented in their letters and journals on the English character of the merchants' houses, the English fashion in dress and even how much English was spoken.[7] The supreme event of the English social calendar was the visit of Lord Nelson and Lady Hamilton for one week in October 1800 as they made their way to London in the wake of Nelson's recent victory over Napoleon at the Battle of the Nile. Heinrich and Johanna were, naturally enough, invited to the Grand Gala arranged in the visitors' honour, but it is uncertain whether they took the twelve-year-old Arthur with them.

With his father devoted to running his business and his mother busy in a social whirl, it is not surprising, and not untypical for families of their class, that young Arthur was brought up largely in the company of nursemaids and servants. He had begun to suffer the anxiety attacks which plagued him thereafter. In his autobiographical notes he recorded that once at the age of six, when his parents were out of the house, he suddenly imagined himself to have been abandoned by them for ever (*mr* iv, p. 507).[8] Perhaps the recent upheaval of the flight from Danzig to Hamburg was a contributory factor, triggering a feeling of homelessness. His early years were punctuated by irregular changes of domicile, for though Hamburg was the place where he mostly lived between the ages of five and nineteen – it was not until he settled in Frankfurt at the age of 45 that he would again have such a permanent address – long periods were spent far away from the city, usually in the company of his parents on one of their many journeys around Europe. One place they never visited was Danzig. Although Johanna was permitted to visit her parents every few years, Heinrich would not lower himself by returning. His will was resolute and authoritative on this, as on everything concerning the family. Arthur's education, which did not formally begin in Hamburg until he was eleven, was inevitably disrupted by the family's travels. But Heinrich's greater purpose was to provide Arthur with opportunities to acquire personal experience, as opposed to indirect acquaintance via books and teachers, of different ways of living, languages and cultures; this, he reasoned, would better fit his son for a future as an international businessman. Heinrich regarded this as 'reading from the book of the world' (G, p. 264), the significance of which – the priority of direct observation over theory – Arthur was later to incorporate into his philosophy.

On 12 June 1797 Arthur's only sister, Louise Adelaide, known as Adele, was born. The following month, during a respite in the conflict between the French and their European neighbours, Arthur was taken by his father on a journey through France as the first stage of his preparation to become a 'man of the world'. After visiting Paris, Heinrich took Arthur to Le Havre to stay with the family of M. Grégoire de Blésimaire, one of his business partners. The two years Arthur spent with the Grégoires he later described as 'by far the happiest part' of his childhood.[9] It is not difficult to understand why. From the letter written to him after he had returned to Hamburg, it seems that M. and Madame Grégoire developed a warmer, more openly affectionate relationship with him than he had with his parents.[10] Schopenhauer wrote that they treated him just like a second son (GB, p. 649). Moreover, in their own son, Anthime, he found a close companion near his own age who became the best friend he ever had, a friendship that lasted well beyond childhood. Arthur and Anthime were taught together by the family tutor, studying a range of subjects including mathematics, Latin and French literature, including Voltaire's poem 'Le Henriade', which attacks religious fanaticism. It was at this time too that Arthur

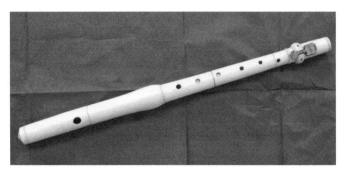

Schopenhauer's ivory flute.

purchased for himself – though not before seeking his father's permission – the ivory flute which was to become a lifelong resource of consolation and joy.

In the spring of 1799 Arthur made the return journey alone by ship to Hamburg, a journey he took pride in not simply because he was aged just eleven but because of the dangers due to the state of near-war currently existing between the European powers. Yet so thoroughly had he immersed himself in the French language and way of life that on reaching home he had, to his father's delight, difficulty in making himself understood in German.

Within months of his return from Le Havre, in the next stage of his father's plans for his education, Arthur was sent to an exclusive private school to learn what would be useful for a merchant to know (*GB*, p. 649). Arthur was fortunate in this choice of his first school, for its headmaster, Dr Johann Heinrich Christian Runge, a Pietist theologian by training, was an enlightened educationalist and an inspirational teacher. Runge eschewed the authoritarianism of other schools, preferring instead 'persuasion and reason, precept and example'.[11] He also believed in fostering a personal relationship with his pupils as well as collaboration with their parents in developing well-educated individuals of sound character. Teaching of Latin and the classics took second place to the modern foreign languages necessary for a European businessman. Runge's fellow teachers also taught geography and topography, mathematics and history, while he himself gave classes in theology in which discussion of moral issues took the place of doctrinal dogmatism. Runge emphasized the importance of 'friendship, kindness, compassion, generosity, charitability, and helping others in business',[12] values which are underwritten by the ethical theory of *The World as Will and Representation.* In later years, writing his *curriculum vitae,* Arthur recorded that for almost four years he enjoyed the teaching in Runge's school 'of this most excellent man and the others' (*GB,* p. 649).

At this point in his life, Arthur was outwardly in conformity with what was expected of someone from the wealthy merchant class. The diaries of his school friends show him indulging in the same rough-and-tumble as they did during school hours. When school was done for the day he became the young gentleman, fencing, horse-riding, playing whist, smoking cigars and drinking and dancing at parties, balls and masquerades. Arthur, it seems, was keen on dancing, though unlike some of his friends he did not find a wife among his partners. But if his schoolmates did not all go on to careers in commerce, they did at least secure positions appropriate to their class.[13] Arthur, however, was slowly nurturing desires that would eventually take his life in a different direction altogether: a direction opposed to his father's wishes and carefully laid plans for him. This was no mere adolescent rebellion against parental pressure. Over the course of his teenage years Arthur found himself drawn more and more towards scholarly pursuits such as classical studies, literature and philosophy. Ironically, it may have been the very freedom and independence of mind that his father had striven to encourage which provided Arthur with the opportunity to discover this tendency in his nature. He was allowed the freedom to roam in his father's library; he encountered from an early age his parents' enthusiasm for the literature and philosophy of France and England; and he was stimulated by the enlightened emphasis on discussion and argument in Runge's theology classes. In fact, Runge supported him in his desire to switch to a Gymnasium when, as was to be expected, Arthur came up against Heinrich's opposition to his son's growing determination to abandon his long-planned career as a merchant.

There surely must have been more than a few family altercations when Arthur's wishes became evident. Heinrich's resolute will and his hopes for the future of his business were such that he could not easily give way. But give way he did, as Arthur explained just over twenty years later in his *curriculum vitae*, written in 1824. Because he associated the life of a scholar with poverty, Heinrich decided, out of fatherly concern for his son, to arrange for Arthur to become a canon at Hamburg cathedral (*GB*, p. 649), a position that would enable him eventually to go on to university.[14] It is bizarre now, in light of the mature Schopenhauer's contempt for the institutions of Christianity, to imagine that he once faced the prospect of being an ecclesiast. In the event, nothing came of the plan, for Heinrich discovered that the cost of purchasing the benefice was prohibitive. In any case, he had contrived another solution to the problem.

In 1803 Heinrich and Johanna were due to take an extensive European tour which would keep them away from Hamburg for almost two years. Arthur was allowed to decide whether or not he would accompany his parents. But his father attached certain conditions to the decision that placed Arthur in a dilemma. If he chose not to take the tour, he could transfer to the Gymnasium and study Latin in preparation for entry to university; if he did choose to go along, then, on his return to Hamburg, he would be apprenticed to a merchant and continue his career in commerce. This was a cruel decision to impose on a fourteen-year-old boy, especially since the tour would allow him to visit his old friends at Le Havre and to see England for the first time. Since he was damned whatever he decided, Arthur – not surprisingly – chose to take the tour. While

Gerhard von Kügelgen's portrait of Schopenhauer aged 15, a watercolour painted in 1803.

this decision temporarily dispelled tensions within the family, in a few years it would burden Arthur with an even more painful conflict.

The Schopenhauers, minus the six-year-old Adele, who was sent to Johanna's parents in Danzig, left Hamburg at the beginning of May 1803. Although Heinrich returned at the end of August 1804, Arthur was not to see Hamburg again until almost 1805.

One wonders at Heinrich's wisdom in leaving his business for so long in a period of such political instability. During the final years of the eighteenth century, Hamburg's trading activities had been constrained by the continuing wars in Europe, bringing the earlier economic boom to an end. In 1801 the city almost lost its vaunted independence when it was occupied by Danish troops, who were finally ousted by pressure from both Prussia and Britain. And although the continuing conflict between France and Britain was formerly concluded with the Peace of Amiens in March 1802, it was not long before both parties had violated the treaty. On the other hand, Heinrich's journey through Europe not only enabled him to renew old business contacts and develop new ones, but made it possible for Arthur to gain the acquaintance of merchants who would be of value to him in his future career as head of the family business. But it may have been that these considerations were, after all, secondary to just getting away and leaving behind the daily routines of home and business, for Heinrich had been showing signs of stress: increasing irritability, absent-mindedness and depression.

The family travelled via Amsterdam to Calais, where they took the last boat to England after news reached the port that war had been declared between France and Britain on 18 May.[15] They arrived in London on 25 May. Arthur was surprised by the scale and vitality of the metropolis as well as by the incessant rain. The family managed to take in all the major tourist attractions the city had to offer. The most glamorous event was a procession of more than a thousand state carriages in celebration of the birthday of King George III. On 8 June Arthur witnessed the hanging of three people, the spectacle of which he considered less shocking than hangings he had seen on the Continent; later that same day he viewed a performance of ventriloquism that aroused his astonishment and admiration. Side-by-side with entries in his diary that recorded the observations and enthusiasms of a typical fifteen-year-old schoolboy are comments indicative of the thoughtful, mature philosopher he became. Thus the sight of the monuments in Westminster Abbey of poets, heroes and kings provoked the reflection that, though death strips them all of their outward, temporal distinctions, it does not touch the greatness of 'their very being', which they take with them beyond the grave.

On 30 June Arthur's sightseeing holiday came to an end. For the next twelve weeks he was a pupil at Revd Thomas Lancaster's Wimbledon School for Young Noblemen and Gentlemen. In the meantime, his parents made a tour of northern England and Scotland. The school had presumably been recommended to the Schopenhauers by their London friends, though perhaps the choice was clinched by the fact of Thomas Lancaster's acquaintance with Lord Nelson.[16] There is a gap in Arthur's diary for his time at the school, but it is evident from his parents' responses, as well as those of his Hamburg friends, to his letters (which have not survived) that he was not happy there. His principal grievance was boredom. Johanna responded, 'Drawing, reading, playing your flute, fencing and going for walks is a good deal of variety, you know. For years I knew hardly any other pleasures, and thrived on it.'[17] Her recommendation to her son comes in the form of a dire warning: 'If you want to . . . accompany us on the rest of our tour, I advise you to make sure that by the time we return your father will have cause to be satisfied with your handwriting, otherwise I cannot be responsible for the consequences.' The threat had its effect, for Arthur arranged for extra writing lessons. His other main complaint can be inferred from his use of the phrase 'infamous bigotry' (*GB*, p. 1), which earned a sharp rebuke from Johanna on the grounds that it was not an expression that should be used by civilized, well-educated people. The expression, with its allusion to Voltaire's notorious '*l'infâme*', manifested Arthur's contemptuous attitude to the dogmatic conservative theology of Revd Thomas Lancaster. That and the authoritarian methods of teaching, which included learning by rote and corporal punishment, must have contrasted badly with the enlightened schooling Arthur had received from Runge. Both of his grievances were aggravated every Sunday when, in addition to numerous Church services and sermons by Thomas Lancaster himself, there was a prohibition on the normal recreational activities, which he listed to one of his friends in Hamburg as 'dancing, singing, whistling, tippling, writing, reading worldly books, playing, shouting, climbing, making a noise, etc.'[18] In fairness, it should be said that Arthur could not have been an easy pupil. Even if his English needed polishing, his fluency in German and French, the breadth of his reading in those languages – he had taken to reading Schiller's tragedies to relieve his boredom – and his first-hand familiarity with people and places in many parts of Europe, as well as his increasing self-confidence in his own intellectual ability, must have made him difficult. Moreover, Arthur was conspicuously lacking in social graces, as his parents never tired of telling him in their letters. His typical demeanour appears to have been one of slouching and shouting. His friends at the school were other German students and he had a number of small but expensive personal items stolen from him. No doubt Arthur's relief on leaving the school on 20 September was matched by that of Revd Lancaster and his associates.

On resuming his diary, Arthur noted that the family had to stay in London longer than they intended since the war between England and France meant there were no boats to Calais. While they hoped each day would be the day of their departure, they did not waste their remaining time. At the theatre, they saw some of the most celebrated actors of the age, including Mrs Sissons and Charles Kemble. They visited the British Museum and St Paul's Cathedral, whose enormous dome Arthur found 'sublime and awe-inspiring', and which he used as an example in his reflections on sublimity in *The World as Will and Representation*. Finally, after fourteen days' enforced delay, on 5 November the Schopenhauers set off for Harwich; from there they took a ship to Rotterdam a few days later.

Arthur never visited Britain again. His five months in England left deep marks on his character. Though he became a lifelong anglophile, he acquired a deep loathing for the narrow-minded bigotry and hypocrisy of Anglican parsons, which he had encountered in the form of Thomas Lancaster, and which he denounced over and over again in his later writings. More important, however, was the fact that he perfected his English. His grasp of the language enabled him to develop a familiarity with English literature, and helped shape his way of writing in German so that it stands pre-eminent among eighteenth- and nineteenth-century German philosophy for its clarity and directness.

The Schopenhauers reached Paris at the end of November and resumed their sightseeing; to Arthur, Paris failed to match up to the spectacle of London. Days were spent at the Louvre, newly enriched by the recent spoils of the Napoleonic campaigns. But for Arthur the highlight was undoubtedly the glimpses of Emperor Napoleon himself at the theatre and on the parade ground. He was also allowed a week to himself to visit his old friends at Le Havre. At the end of January the family continued its tour through the towns and cities of southern France, eventually heading homewards by way of Lyon, Geneva, Vienna and Berlin.

In a notebook entry of 1832 Arthur remarked that 'when I was in my seventeenth year, without any proper schooling, I was affected by the misery and wretchedness of life, as was the Buddha when in his youth he caught sight of sickness, old age, pain and death' (*MR* IV, p. 119). On the evidence of his travel diary, it was the situation of the miserable galley slaves in the arsenal at Toulon which moved him most. Their situation struck him as more terrible than a death sentence.[19] Given Arthur's tendency, in Johanna's words, to 'brood on the misery of human beings', such experiences led him to think of the world not as 'the work of an all-bountiful, infinitely good being, but rather of a devil who had summoned into existence creatures in order to gloat over the sight of their anguish and agony' (*MR* IV, p. 119). In total contrast were the ecstatic experiences he enjoyed while travelling through and climbing among the Alps of France and Switzerland, which he eloquently described in his diary.[20] These experiences, too, were formative: his love of the beauty of nature manifests itself throughout his writings, while hiking and country walks became lifelong passions.

The European tour came to an end in late August 1804, when on their departure from Berlin Heinrich returned to Hamburg, while Johanna and Schopenhauer travelled to Danzig. There Johanna visited her relatives and Arthur was confirmed in the Marienkirche where he had been baptized. Having enjoyed fifteen months of mostly 'reading in the book of the world', it was now time for Arthur to keep his promise to his father by beginning his commercial career. He was first apprenticed to a respected Danzig merchant, Jacob Kabrun, one of Heinrich's old friends. In his letters from Hamburg during the autumn of 1804 – the last Arthur received from his father – Heinrich mixed stern criticism of the remaining monstrosities in Arthur's handwriting with the exhortation that he should walk with a straight back and not get round shoulders, and worldly advice about the importance of learning how to write business letters.[21] References to flute-playing, dancing and riding suggest that Arthur was making the most of his leisure time away from the tedium of the counting house. And although Heinrich was reluctant to give his son any credit, it seems that Johanna had heard that Arthur was at last turning into a nicely behaved young gentleman.

Early in January 1805 Arthur began an apprenticeship with Senator Jenisch in Hamburg, though initially he was required by his father to attend Dr Runge's morning classes in theology. Gradually, the awful reality of his situation became evident. As he later put it, 'my whole nature struggled against this trade' (*GB*, p. 651). Realizing the mistake he had made, he despaired of ever getting free from his hateful occupation. He began to neglect his duties, striving to find ways to read the books he craved, either illicitly at the

The Port of Hamburg on the River Elbe as it looked in Schopenhauer's day.

counting house or at home in the evenings, and he deceitfully took time away from the office in order to attend lectures by Franz Gall, the controversial phrenologist. Some kind of crash was inevitable. But then, on the morning of 20 April, his father was found dead. Heinrich had drowned in the canal behind the family home, having fallen from the loft in the warehouse. It is likely that the fall was deliberate. Officially, the death was regarded as a tragic accident, but both Johanna and Arthur understood Heinrich's death to be suicide, though they did not openly acknowledge this to one another. Heinrich had been ailing for some time. Clues to his declining vitality and increasing anxiety can be found in Johanna's letters to Arthur when he was at school in Wimbledon: 'you know that your father does not like meeting people . . .'; 'you know how your father manufactures worries when he has no real ones'.[22] The deterioration continued after his return to Hamburg, with memory lapses and outbursts of anger, his condition compounded by his growing deafness and the stress brought on by the difficulties facing his business as a result of the Continental Blockade, the Napoleonic embargo against trade with Britain. Arthur never forgave his mother for what he saw as her neglect of his father in his illness, and his bitterness towards her, which would erupt into dreadful quarrelling in later years, worked like a poison through his life to disfigure his relationships with and attitude to women. His father, whom he both revered and feared with all the intensity of adolescence, Arthur held blameless, and in his later philosophical reflections he always argued that suicide should be seen as an irrationality rather than an action to be condemned.

Heinrich's sudden death liberated Johanna. Not yet 40, still vivacious and ambitious and with a substantial inheritance, she was free to fashion her own future. By contrast, Heinrich's death did not release Arthur from servitude but served only to tighten the shackles. In honour of the memory of his beloved father, Arthur felt more strongly than ever his obligation to keep the promise he had made to pursue the vocation his father had desired for him. As a consequence his intellectual interests and yearnings for a scholar's education came loaded with feelings of guilt. In his grief over losing his father and his despair at the hopelessness of his predicament, he gave way, as he admitted in later life, to bouts of depression (*GB*, p. 651).

Within months of Heinrich's death Johanna sold the mansion on Neuer Wandrahm and instigated the liquidation of the family business. She wished to turn her back on the commercial environ-ment in which she had spent most of her life. In May 1806 she visited Weimar, the small provincial capital of the Duchy of Saxe-Weimar which, with Goethe as its presiding genius, was one of the significant cultural centres in Europe. Here she hoped that she might be able to realize her secretly cherished ambition of becom-ing an author herself in the course of participating in the city's literary salons. On the morning of 21 September Johanna and Adele departed for Weimar before Arthur found the letter informing him that she had left Hamburg forever.[23] Even though he knew her departure was imminent, the abruptness and secrecy must have come as a shock. Johanna wrote that she disliked farewells and she reminded her son of 'how any violent emotion' affected her; but it was perhaps his emotion rather than her own that she sought to avoid.

Deprived of his family home, Arthur was obliged to take lodgings in a boarding-house. Some verses written at this time express in religious cliché the the bitter anguish he felt at the contrast between his aspirations and the everyday circumstances of his life.

What greater advantage
Than to triumph entirely
Over a life so hollow and vain
That can ne'er fulfil our wish,
Though yearning breaks our hearts.
How fine 'twould be lightly and softly
To wander through the wastes of life on earth
Our feet untrammelled by its dust,
Our gaze unaverted from heaven. (*MR* I, p. 2)

This manifestation of adolescent yearning to escape the drabness of daily existence and find something finer and purer carries traces of Lutheran Pietism and the works of the German Romantics, in which Arthur was immersed at this period. Perhaps it was to help him overcome the starkness of the Pietist contrast between the sinful world and the world of God that his father had given him a pamphlet by Matthias Claudius entitled *To My Son* (1799). The journalist and poet Claudius, who had become a friend of Klopstock and had lived in Hamburg at the end of his life, argued that true piety was to be found not in scornful rejection of the world but in a reconciliation of worldly necessities and spiritual demands, a compromise that would preserve the integrity of the inner self in the face of the external world. Arthur kept his copy of this book until his death, and made use of Claudius' writings in the late essays collected in *Parerga und Paralipomena* and in the third edition of *The World as Will and Representation*. But it was the traditional Pietist characterization of human life as a vale of tears that Arthur endorsed in his mature philosophy of existence in space and time. And it was the wretchedness of ordinary life, the centuries of barbarism, the numberless minutes consuming everything worthwhile, that he bemoaned in a series of letters to Johanna in Weimar. He took refuge in art and, in particular, in music – his flute-playing was now a daily routine.

> Beloved art, in how many a bleak hour,
> When I am enmeshed in life's tumultuous round,
> Have you kindled my heart to the warmth of love,
> And borne me away to a better world.[24]

The Romanticist exaltation of music as something divine which, according to Wilhelm Wackenroder (whose essays Arthur was reading), reveals all the emotions of our souls in a language unknown to us in ordinary life made a deep impression on him, as did Wackenroder's figure of the artistic genius who transcends all academic rules.[25]

A temporary relief from the grind of Arthur's daily life came when his boyhood friend from Le Havre, Anthime, arrived in Hamburg in May 1806 to complete his own training as a merchant, a career that Anthime, like Arthur, regarded as completely stupid and useless. Arthur introduced Anthime to the novels and stories of the Romantic writers, Ludwig Tieck (who also edited the essays of Wackenroder) and Jean Paul, as well as recommending heavier reading such as Schiller's *The History of the Secession of the United Netherlands from Spanish Rule*.[26] It was not long before they were sharing lodgings and taking hiking trips to the forests near Trittau in Holstein. On finishing their days' work, the two friends, free from parental discipline, explored the numerous temptations that Hamburg had to offer young men of their wealth and class. But Anthime, to Arthur's dismay, was more successful in their pursuit of socially inferior women than Arthur, who lacked the open-hearted affability of his 'French brother'. This life of indulgence further contributed to Arthur's spiritual torment, to which he gave exaggerated expression in verse.

> Voluptuous pleasure, infernal delight,
> Love insatiable and invincible!
> From the heights of heaven
> Thou hast dragged me down
> And cast me in fetters
> Into the dust of this earth.
> How shall I aspire and soar
> To the throne of the eternal . . . (*MR* I, p. 1)

On reading of her son's unhappiness in his chosen career, Johanna tended at first to attribute it to the melancholic disposition he had inherited from his father. She questioned the seriousness of Arthur's desire to change his vocation, contrasting the privileges to be enjoyed as a rich merchant with the modest lifestyle of a scholar. And yet, having sold off Heinrich's company, Johanna had already unlocked the door of Arthur's prison: since there was no family business for him to take control of, it was unnecessary for him to become a merchant.[27] There remained the question of Arthur's suitability for academic study. Thanks to Heinrich's arrangements for his son's upbringing, Arthur at the age of nineteen lacked the basic grammar school training normally required for progress in higher education. Here Arthur benefited from his mother's easy sociability, which he disparaged as frivolity. Among the many literary and academic acquaintances Johanna soon made after her arrival in

Weimar, she was befriended by Karl Ludwig Fernow, a distinguished art critic and archaeologist, and at that time librarian to the Dowager Duchess Anna Amalia. Fernow himself had undergone a dramatic change of vocation earlier in his life, having initially worked as a clerk and an apprentice pharmacist. After listening to his opinion that, to someone of sufficient talent and determination, inexperience in formal school training and classical languages need not be an insuperable obstacle to higher study, Johanna wrote to Arthur at the end of April 1807 laying before him in some detail the nature of the choice he had to make. She emphasized that it was entirely his decision: she would not advise him.[28] Enclosed with her own letter was a note of encouragement and wise counsel from Fernow. On reading this, Arthur broke down in tears (*G*, p. 382). He lost no time in submitting his resignation of his apprenticeship and in making preparations to leave Hamburg for Gotha, where, on Fernow's recommendation, he was to enter the Gymnasium to prepare himself for his new vocation as a scholar.

2

A High Mountain Road

Philosophical genius sometimes manifests itself early in a writer's life. David Hume famously completed his masterpiece, *A Treatise of Human Nature*, in 1737 when he was only 26. Wittgenstein finished the *Tractatus Logico-Philosophicus* in 1918 at the age of 29. A hundred years earlier, Arthur Schopenhauer was 30 when he finished his magnum opus, *The World as Will and Representation*, in 1818. And yet in 1807 Schopenhauer was a teenager lacking a classical education and employed as a merchant's apprentice. Within eleven years he prepared himself for a university education, acquired a Doctorate in Philosophy, published a theory of colour which challenged the work of Goethe, and wrote what was to become one of the most influential philosophical works of the nineteenth century. By any standards, his progress and achievement are astonishing.

Hamburg had been under French occupation for over six months when Schopenhauer left for Gotha, twenty miles from Weimar, towards the end of May 1807. Unlike the great city he left behind, Gotha was a small and sleepy town dominated by the ducal court at the Schloss Friedenstein. As in all such provincial towns, gossip, snobbery and petty rivalries were endemic. Schopenhauer mocked these disagreeable habits in a short poem called the 'Philistines of Gotha' shortly after his arrival, noting that

No event is unobserved,
No cat can walk upon the roof
Without their coming to know of it.

The poem is not a manifestation of a city boy's dismay at provincial
habits so much as an attempt by Schopenhauer to distance himself
from his new neighbours. Distinguished as he was by considerable
wealth, he also now though of himself as one of the enlightened few
in the midst of the philistine many.

At the mind, thoughts and worth of man
They do not prick up their ears. (*MR* I, p. 3)

Schopenhauer was, after all, a student at 'the flourishing and
famous' Gymnasium, boarding in the house of one of its teachers
and receiving private tuition in Latin (*GB*, p. 651).

Small it might have been, yet Gotha was famous in enlightened
circles, its reputation due both to the fact that figures of the eminence
of Voltaire had been resident at court there, and to the distinction
of the teachers at the Gymnasium. It was from the headmaster
himself, F. W. Döring, the well-known Latinist, that Schopenhauer
received additional lessons in Latin; and the classics master,
Friedrich Jacobs, who was a friend of Johanna's acquaintance
Karl Fernow, was a scholar in contact with many famous names
in the literary world. Schopenhauer had a high regard for these
men, even affection, which he expressed in the valedictory ode
he composed for Jacobs on his departure for Bavaria.

So long frustrated, Schopenhauer now poured his energy and
passion into his studies. Owing to his lack of knowledge of classical
languages, he was only able to attend classes in German. But his
essays earned praise from Jacobs. Twice daily he received tuition in
Latin and, by his own account, his progress was so impressive that
Döring predicted a splendid career for him. Schopenhauer's

despondency and doubt about his future were replaced by increasing optimism that he could achieve his goal of a life in scholarship. With growing confidence in his own abilities, he indulged the extrovert side of his nature. Being somewhat older and more mature, more 'a man of the world', he revelled in the attention of his fellow students. He began to socialize in aristocratic circles, to the consternation of his mother. In a few weeks he spent considerable sums of the money from his mother's allowance on elegant clothing, excursions and hired horses, and dined extravagantly. But the bubble soon burst. To amuse his school friends, Schopenhauer composed a sarcastic verse about one of the masters, who was not one of Schopenhauer's teachers. When the incident came to Döring's attention, he cancelled Schopenhauer's private tuition. Unable to bear this slight from a respected figure, and someone, moreover, whose good opinion was vital to his still fragile sense of his own worth, Schopenhauer determined to leave the Gymnasium at the end of the term. He informed his mother that he would continue his education at Weimar.

Johanna was understandably alarmed by this news, though, judging by her letters, more at the prospect of Schopenhauer coming to live with her than she was at his leaving the Gymnasium. By this time Johanna had through her own resourcefulness established a place for herself at the centre of Weimar's cultural life. She was now accustomed to living as an independent woman, arranging her life in accordance with her own decisions instead of at the demands of her husband. She regarded Schopenhauer's arrival in her household as a threat to her independence; for he, with Henrich's temperament and conscious of himself as his father's son and heir, was inclined to treat Johanna as a woman subservient to his masculine will. She did not hesitate to speak plainly, declaring that she would make any sacrifice to avoid their living together. Schopenhauer's scowling face, ill-humour and oracular judgements brooking no contradiction distressed her and upset the tranquillity of the way of life she had established. And, she reminded him, his earlier visits had resulted in violent scenes about nothing.[1] Johanna's solution to their predicament was that Schopenhauer should take lodgings in Weimar and be a welcome guest, under certain conditions, in her home. The conditions she laid down were that he should not interfere in her domestic arrangements or in matters concerning Adele's health and education. Schopenhauer could visit her every day from one to three p.m. and stay for the evening on her two 'social days', which he was welcome to attend, provided he refrained from 'tiresome arguing' and lamentations on 'the stupid world and human misery' which gave her nightmares.[2] Schopenhauer accepted his mother's conditions and moved into lodgings in Weimar towards the end of December 1807.

Johanna's anxiety over Schopenhauer's behaviour while visiting on her 'social days' reflected the respect in which she was held in Weimar society. Her position had been achieved in circumstances of great adversity. Her journey with the ten-year-old Adele from Hamburg to Weimar in September 1806 had coincided with the outbreak of war between Prussia and France. Within weeks of her arrival Weimar was occupied by French troops under orders from Napoleon to take revenge for the decision of Karl August, Duke of Saxony-Weimar, to support the Prussians. Having survived the ordeal, Johanna wrote letters on 18 and 19 October to Schopenhauer in Hamburg outlining the dreadful events she had lived through. 'You see I am still alive', she began. During the bombardment, on the night following the Battle of Jena (14 October), Johanna and Adele huddled together on the sofa while 'the cannon thundered, the floor shook and the windows rattled': she hoped that 'a single ball might kill us both'. In the burning town the French soldiery went on the rampage. Johanna prepared herself as best she could. Her valuable possessions were hidden throughout the house, wisely 'taking care not to strip the house in such a manner as to arouse suspicion'; her remaining cash and her jewellery were sewn into

Caroline Bardua, *Johanna Schopenhauer and her Daughter Adele*, 1806, oil on canvas.

her own and her housemaid's undergarments; food and wine were
made available for the expected intruders. In the common peril,
the niceties of social convention were cast aside when hard-pressed
members of the Weimar community sought refuge in her home.
During the night French guards burst into the house, their sabres
drawn, their uniforms spattered in blood. These terrifying men
were unexpectedly placated by the sight of the ten-year-old Adele in
her nightdress, who had been awoken by their noise. This allowed
Johanna and her maid, both French speakers, the opportunity to
arrange the soldiers' peaceful departure with supplies of food and

wine. Other residents of Weimar were less fortunate than Johanna. When the French eventually left the town, she said they left behind 'an abyss of suffering . . . things that would make your [Arthur's] hair stand on end'.[3] Side-by-side with other members of Weimar society, she played her part in alleviating the suffering and helped restore normal life.

The shared tribulations of the occupation and its aftermath had enabled Johanna to establish personal relationships in a matter of days that she might otherwise have struggled to achieve at all. And none was more important than her friendship with Goethe, at that time the pre-eminent figure in European culture as well as a Councillor of the Ducal Court. It was Goethe himself who told Johanna that the baptism of fire had made her into a Weimarian. The same fire had forged new relationships for Goethe. He had scandalized Weimar society since 1788 by openly living with his mistress, Christiane Vulpius, a former factory worker, who bore him a son in 1789. It was only his intimacy with the Duke himself that enabled Goethe to maintain his position in the community. He committed a further outrage to convention the day after the French occupation ended by marrying Christiane in tribute to her selfless bravery in defending him and his property from the marauding troops. Johanna, who had been introduced to Goethe before the occupation and had become further acquainted with him in its aftermath, was the first in Weimar to receive Goethe and his new wife into her home. As she reported to Schopenhauer, 'I think if Goethe could give her his name then we can surely give her a cup of tea.'[4] The next day, Johanna took up Christiane's invitation to call on her. Perhaps it was partly Johanna's status as a comparative stranger in Weimar that made it easier for Goethe to introduce Christiane to her as his wife. Yet his frequent visits to Johanna's home attest to his appreciation of her own personal qualities. As a star of Weimar society, Goethe's presence soon attracted other notable figures to Johanna's 'social days' – and not

Joseph Karl Stieler, *Johann Wolfgang von Goëthe* (aged 79), 1828, oil on canvas.

merely the social elite of Weimar. Goethe was a kind of intellectual and cultural magnet who drew writers, artists, scholars and scientists, as well as assorted celebrities, to Weimar from across Europe. Naturally, she did not wish these personalities to be disturbed by the moods and outbursts of her gauche son. Yet it was amongst the distinguished intellectuals he later met in Johanna's salon that he received encouragement and stimulation vital to the development of his philosophy.

A few months before Schopenhauer's arrival in the town, Goethe had brought to Weimar the young philologist Franz Passow, and appointed him Professor of Greek Literature at the Gymnasium. Less than two years older than Schopenhauer, Passow had studied classics under Jacobs at Gotha and went on to become one of Germany's greatest classical philologists.[5] It was through her friendship with Goethe that Johanna was able to secure Passow as a tutor for Schopenhauer, who was now in need of private tuition, as the news of his disgrace at Gotha proved an obstacle to his entering the Gymnasium in Weimar. With preparation for university entrance as his goal, Schopenhauer pursued independently his study of mathematics and history, while Passow was responsible for continuing his education in the classical languages, eventually concentrating on Greek when his pupil had demonstrated his excellence in Latin. Passow was a member of the Neoclassical movement in eighteenth- and nineteenth-century Germany, which was committed to the study of ancient Greece. It had been initiated by the art historian and archaeologist Johann Joachim Winckelmann and was promoted by the writings of Goethe and Schiller. The Neoclassical movement inspired the Romantic poetry and music of the early nineteenth century with a vision of a lost golden era in human culture. Greek studies, it was argued, would not only provide the foundations of proper education but, by displacing the dominance of the Bible, would provide an impetus to the reformation of the nation's political and cultural institutions. Passow communicated his enthusiasm to his precocious student, whose devotion to classical learning was unshakeable. As Schopenhauer put it in a late essay, 'The ancients will never become obsolete . . . Discredit and disgrace await the age that dares to set aside the ancients' (*PP* II, p. 404).

During this period of study in Weimar, Schopenhauer developed the habit of using manuscript books in which to keep notes on the subjects of his studies as well as set down his reflections on life.[6] In the earliest of these is a continuation of the contrast found in his poetical lampoon of the philistines of Gotha between the 'mind, thoughts and worth of man' and the trivial interests that engage most people. For example, a waiter, who spends most of his days worrying over trivial details, is nonetheless, as a human being, the noblest of creatures. However, among the dull masses of humanity, there are a few distinguished men whose lives are not dominated by corporeal demands and who are able to detect a spiritual world, 'the invisible in the visible', from which they can view everyday affairs with 'the greatest calm and unconcern'. In the absence of the spiritual, without 'the few moments of religion, art and pure love', there would be nothing in life except triviality (*MR*, I, pp. 4–9).

At this stage of his development the vestiges of the religion of Schopenhauer's upbringing disposed him to think of the spiritual dimension of existence in relation to a deity. The idea of a boundless infinity with no consciousness external to man's was 'a terrible thought' (*MR*, I, p. 8). Yet his awareness of suffering had already led him to speculate whether the world was the creation of a devilish rather than a wholly good being, and now he began to systematically question the orthodox conception of the deity. If we assume that all things are not perfect, then

> two other cases only are possible; either we must, unless we assume everything to be for an evil purpose, concede power to the good will as well as to the bad, the latter forcing the former to work in a round-about way, *or* we must attribute this power only to chance and hence to a want of perfection to the will that guides and directs the arrangement or control of things. (*MR*, I, p. 9)

This philosophically sophisticated argument is impressive for a teenager who had had no formal training in philosophy. Schopenhauer's solution to the problem of evil in the world is for individuals to refrain from egoistically shuffling their own suffering onto others, which only increases the quantity of suffering by adding to 'the original positive evil (the guilt of the world)'. But if individuals voluntarily take suffering on themselves, then evil is reduced to the smallest possible amount 'and the Kingdom of God will come to pass' (*MR*, I, pp. 9–10). While the thinking here is inchoate, Hübscher is right in saying that these are 'the building blocks of Schopenhauer's ethics'.[7]

It is easy to appreciate how uncomfortable Schopenhauer must have felt during his twice-weekly attendances at his mother's social gatherings. Not only was he in the presence of many distinguished men, some of whom, such as Goethe and the poet Christoph Martin Wieland, he idolized, but he was also prohibited by Johanna's strict conditions from indulging his passion for argument. To make things worse, he was completely ignored by Goethe, as indeed he was by most of the other eminent visitors. And unfortunately for Schopenhauer, Karl Fernow, Johanna's closest friend and the man whose advice had been so invaluable in setting him on the path of his chosen vocation, died the year following Schopenhauer's arrival in Weimar.[8] He later confided to a friend that he 'always felt strange and lonely' in relation to his mother and her circle (*G*, p. 130). These experiences aggravated his natural tendency to anxiety and sense of isolation. He expressed some of this in verse after undergoing another of his recurrent panic attacks.

> In the depth of a tempestuous night I awoke in great alarm . . .
> But neither glimmer nor faintest ray
> Could pierce the inky darkness.
> Solid and impenetrable was it spread
> As if it could to no sun yield.
> I thought that day would never come.
> A mighty fear lay hold of me, I felt afraid, alone and forsaken . . .
> (*MR*, I, p. 5)

Schopenhauer did become friendly with two of Johanna's guests, Johannes Daniel Falk and Friedrich Zacharias Werner. Falk, who had been made Legation Councillor in 1806, was a philanthropist and writer of plays and satires. It was with Falk that Schopenhauer travelled in the autumn of 1808 the short distance to Erfurt where Napoleon had summoned many of the crowned heads and nobility of Europe for the Congress to reaffirm with Tsar Alexander I the alliance between France and Russia. Goethe, too, was summoned for a private audience with Napoleon in recognition of the fact that, as Wieland put it, he was in the world of poetry what Napoleon was in the world of politics. The splendour of the occasion failed to impress Schopenhauer, who disparaged the court ladies for their shallowness in regarding Napoleon beforehand as a monster and afterwards as 'the most charming man in the world' (*G*, p. 21). Schopenhauer was already enthusiastic about the work of Zacharias Werner, the celebrated Romantic dramatist, when he, like Schopenhauer, arrived in Weimar at the end of 1807. Schopenhauer enjoyed his company, and in later life remembered that in their many conversations Werner even spoke 'seriously and philosophically' (*G*, p. 20). His friendship with Werner provided further motivation for his attendance at Weimar's theatre, where Schopenhauer had developed a crush on Karoline Jagemann, one of Germany's great actresses and singers. As the mistress of none other than Duke Karl August, she was evidently unattainable, if not unapproachable; and he portrayed himself, in suitably maudlin verse, standing underneath her window on a wintry morning in the hope she might appear there and see him gazing up (*MR*, I, pp. 6–7).

The year 1809 was an important one in Schopenhauer's life. On 22 February he came of age and was entitled to assume control of his share of his father's estate, which had been divided equally between Johanna and the two children. He received approximately 19,000 thalers, together with a part-interest in the family properties in the vicinity of Danzig. Johanna tried to persuade Schopenhauer to follow her and invest his capital with the Danzig banker A. L. Muhl at an attractive rate of 8 per cent. Being more cautious and with a better head for business than his mother, Schopenhauer deposited 6,000 thalers with Muhl and the rest in government bonds. All told, the annual income from his inheritance was almost 1,000 thalers, which was more than double the salary for a well-paid professor at

Alfred Krausse, *Arthur Schopenhauer in his 21st Year*, 1809; an engraving after a watercolour by Karl Ludwig Kaaz.

the nearby university of Jena'.[9] Schopenhauer's dream of a life devoted to scholarship was now within his grasp.

Schopenhauer addressed his academic studies with intense concentration and relentless determination. He made such progress that by the autumn of 1809, his tutor, Passow, was able to assure him that his work had adequately prepared him for entry to a university. Accordingly, Schopenhauer enrolled at the University of Göttingen. He chose not to attend the distinguished university of Jena, perhaps because of its closeness to Weimar: after two years' immersion in the cultivated culture of Weimar, he needed a fresh intellectual atmosphere. More importantly, whereas Jena was well past its prime as the centre of Idealist philosophy and Romantic poetry, Göttingen had established itself as a thoroughly modern university with a reputation for scientific exploration and research. It was in medicine, not philosophy, that Schopenhauer enrolled himself as a student. He chose medicine for the reason that it would provide him with a thorough introduction to the scientific study of mankind. In this respect Schopenhauer was keeping faith with the spirit of his upbringing, so carefully organized by his father: he would employ experience and observation in establishing facts before indulging in theory and speculation. He would later make this explicit in his view that no one should undertake metaphysics 'without having acquired a knowledge of all the branches of natural science' (*WWR* II, pp. 178–9).

Determined to make up for his lack of formal schooling, Schopenhauer took classes in a wide range of subjects at Göttingen, including Constitutional History, European History and History of the Crusades, Ethnography, Physics, Chemistry, Mathematics, Botany, Mineralogy, Physiology and Comparative Anatomy, and Natural History. He took four courses with the eminent physiologist and anthropologist Johann Friedrich Blumenbach, who was one of the first to study mankind as an aspect of natural history. Schopenhauer's respect for his teacher expressed in a late essay on religion in which he writes warmly of Blumenbach's ethical concern for animal welfare and for his awareness of the horrors of vivisection (*PP*, II, p. 373), an issue on which Schopenhauer came to feel very strongly. At Göttingen Schopenhauer was able to indulge his love of passionate argument with a small group of friends, one of whom, Karl Josias von Bunsen, a future German diplomat and scholar, used terms such as 'rough', 'heated', 'spiky' and 'sulky' to describe Schopenhauer's debating style.[10] Other friends included William Backhouse Astor, son of John (born Johann) Jacob Astor, the American millionaire fur trader (originally from Waldorf), as well as former acquaintances from Gotha and Weimar. Schopenhauer did not take much part in the wilder social life of the student fraternity, notorious for its drinking parties, gambling and duelling, a practice he held to be both contemptible and absurd (see, for example, *PP* 1, pp. 386ff). He preferred to order his days around concentrated application to his studies, resorting to his flute and walking his pet poodle for relaxation. Schopenhauer later wrote of this time that his greater maturity and broader experience, as well as his radically different nature, had led him into seclusion and loneliness (*GB*, p. 653). In this respect, he was forming habits of mind and behaviour that would structure his life from this time onwards.

During the course of his first year at Göttingen, Schopenhauer began to consider changing his focus from medicine to philosophy. The evidence of his notebooks from his time in Weimar indicates that even then his thinking was tending in a philosophical direction, and during his second semester at Göttingen he began to borrow philosophical works by Schelling and Plato from the university library. In his *curriculum vitae* of 1824 he wrote that he made his decision to devote himself exclusively to philosophy after he had gained some reasonable knowledge of himself and also of the subject (*G*, p. 653). It was at the beginning of his second year as a student, in the autumn of 1810, that Schopenhauer transferred to the study of philosophy. Six months later, on a visit to Weimar during the Easter holidays, he spoke to the 78-year-old poet Wieland, who told him bluntly that philosophy was not a solid field of study. Schopenhauer's reply gives some insight into his decision. 'Life', he said, 'is a disagreeable thing. I have set myself to spend it in thinking about it' (*G*, p. 22). Impressed by this reply, Wieland told the young man he had acted correctly; and to Johanna he forecast that something great would one day come of this man.

Schopenhauer's first teacher in philosophy was Gottlob Ernst Schulze (1761–1833) who, while at the University of Helmstedt in 1792, had published *Aenesidemus*, a response to the fundamental doctrines of Kant's critical philosophy. He was among the first generation of academic philosophers who had to come to terms with the legacy of the great Copernican Revolution in philosophy, which Kant had inaugurated in his *Critique of Pure Reason* of 1781. The most significant impact was registered at Jena, where philosophers such as Fichte, Hegel and Schelling critically developed aspects of Kant's philosophy, each in his own way, thereby giving rise to the movement known as Absolute Idealism which envisaged reality as universal, God-like self-consciousness. Schulze's reaction was to defend scepticism concerning our knowledge of physical objects against Kant's attempted refutation and to expose flaws in Kant's own methodology.

Schulze had a great influence on the character of Schopenhauer's own philosophical thinking, for he advised him to study the philosophy of Plato and Kant before all others, something Schopenhauer began to do during the session of 1810–11. Schopenhauer's earliest surviving notes on his reading of Plato and Kant make clear that he had doubts about Kant's critical philosophy, whereas he felt an immediate affinity with the mystical side of Plato's philosophy, which identifies reality with the transcendent world of changeless Forms or Ideas, and which Kant had argued was unknowable. In striking contrast to his later estimation of *The Critique of Pure Reason*, he maintained that Kant's regulative use of reason (*Vernunft*) was perhaps the worst miscarriage of the human mind, tantamount to the suicide of philosophy (*MR* I, p. 12). What Schopenhauer finds objectionable in Kant, as is evident from the contrast he draws between Kant and Plato, is the restriction Kant places upon the capacity of human understanding, confining it within the bounds of possible experience; whereas Plato ascertains 'true depth' by treating objects of experience as 'letters in which he reads the divine Ideas' (*MRI*, p. 12). He conceded that Kant is acute and clever but argued that what is missing is the spiritual dimension which is so pronounced in Plato. These two philosophers soon became for Schopenhauer not only the pinnacles of philosophical achievement against which he measured the work of others, including himself, but, eventually, the twin foundations of his great philosophical system. As he put it in the very first sentence of his doctoral thesis, *The Fourfold Root of the Principle of Sufficient Reason*, 'The divine Plato and the marvellous Kant unite their firm and impressive voices in recommending a rule for the method of all philosophizing, indeed of all knowledge in general' (*FR*, p. 1).

Like his notes on Schulze's recommended reading, those Schopenhauer made on the lectures by Schulze he attended contain germs of ideas that flourished in his final philosophical system. But as well as displaying his initial reflections on what his teachers had to say, his notes also reveal responses that are indicative of deep-seated aspects of his personality. For example, in his notes on Schulze's lectures on psychology given during the autumn/winter semester of 1810–11, Schopenhauer suddenly explodes into abuse, calling his teacher a 'blockhead' and an 'infernal brute' (*MR* II, p. 14). This is an early and comparatively mild example of the intemperate language Schopenhauer was frequently to employ later in his career when criticizing distinguished academic figures. On this occasion at least, he condescends to ask himself why he is so abusive today when he suffers in silence every other day. Suffering in silence was something Schopenhauer found difficult, especially on issues about which he felt he had a right to speak up. This was, of course, the very problem his mother complained of; and it was this problem that ensured that Schopenhauer found himself without close companionship throughout most of his life. But by now he was coming to see that for him a life devoted to philosophy meant nothing less than solitude. He captured his sense of the difficulty in a brilliant rhetorical passage which weaves his teenage experience of climbing among the Alps into the Platonic myth of the philosopher leaving the cave in pursuit of the vision of the Idea of Goodness.

Philosophy is a high mountain road which is reached only by a steep path covered with sharp stones and prickly thorns. It is an isolated road and becomes ever more desolate, the higher we ascend. Whoever pursues this path must show no fear, but must leave everything behind and confidently make his own way in the wintry snow . . . He soon sees the world beneath him . . . its jarring sounds no longer reach his ear . . . He himself is always in the pure cool mountain air and now beholds the sun when all below is still engulfed in dead of night (*MR* I, p. 14).

After taking Schulze's course in logic during the summer semester of 1811, Schopenhauer felt that he needed to continue his philosophical journey by leaving Göttingen. He decided upon the University of Berlin. Founded in 1810 by the liberal educational reformer and linguist Wilhelm von Humboldt, the university (now known as the Humboldt University of Berlin) had already attracted a glittering array of distinguished intellectuals, including the philosopher-theologian Friedrich Daniel Schleiermacher, the zoologist Martin Heinrich Lichtenstein and the Greek scholar Friedrich August Wolf. But these notable figures were not the principal attraction for Schopenhauer: that was Johann Gottlieb Fichte, one of the leading philosophers of the day and a founder of German idealism. As Schopenhauer explained in a letter of 1851, he moved to Berlin in the expectation that in Fichte he would become acquainted with 'a genuine philosopher and a great mind' (*GB*, p. 261). With these high hopes, Schopenhauer travelled to Berlin, not via Weimar but instead on the high road through the Hartz mountains.

3

Dr Schopenhauer

When Schopenhauer enrolled at the University of Berlin in the autumn of 1811, he was a comparative newcomer to the discipline of philosophy, having spent just one year formally studying the subject. Two years later he had completed the doctoral dissertation *On the Fourfold Root of the Principle of Sufficient Reason*, which was the foundation of the philosophical system that he worked on for the next five years. But this intense intellectual activity took place under the shadow of war. Schopenhauer was compelled more than once to uproot in order to avoid being engulfed by the conflict. His overriding concern was to complete the philosophical work he felt that he alone was capable of creating. As he said in his letter accompanying the submission of his dissertation,

> When, in the early summer of this year [1813], the noise of war drove the Muses from Berlin, where I was studying philosophy . . . I, who had sworn allegiance to their colours alone, likewise left the city with their retinue . . . because I was most deeply pervaded by the conviction that I was not born to serve mankind with my fist but with my head . . . (*GB*, p. 643)[1]

Berlin had been the capital city of Prussia from the beginning of the eighteenth century and a centre of the European Enlightenment since the reign of Frederick the Great. But after the devastating defeat at the the Battle of Jena, Prussia was stripped of almost half its territory and obliged to pay punitive war reparations. In the wake of this humiliating disaster Frederick William III declared that 'the State must make up in intellectual force what she has lost in physical'. Granted self-government by Napoleon, Berlin took the lead in the modernization of the state through a series of political, educational and cultural reforms. Among the most significant of these was the root-and-branch reorganization of the educational system in accordance with the new ideas of the Swiss educationalist Johann Pestalozzi, who maintained that education should be available to the masses, not just the elite few, as an essential part of their development into more complete human beings.[2] Consequently, adult literacy rose steadily among the German population, reaching 50 per cent by 1840,[3] a development that played a part in Schopenhauer's rise to fame in the 1850s. The apex of the new educational structure was the creation in 1810 of the University of Berlin, which was intended to so unite the learned institutions that the partnership of scholarship and science would provide a moral force within the state and so revive the spirit of the whole German nation. Fittingly, Fichte, the university's first professor of philosophy, whose *Addresses to the German Nation* in the winter of 1807–8 (published 1808) were an early rallying call for the unification of Germany, was elected Rector in October 1811, just weeks before Schopenhauer arrived to begin his studies.

Schopenhauer had little sympathy with the reinvigoration of the Prussian state or, indeed, with the unification of Germany. For one thing, as a five-year-old he had been a victim of Prussian aggression when his family was compelled to flee their home in Danzig. For another, he was, unusually for a German philosopher in the first half of the nineteenth century, singularly uninterested in political philosophy. The state, for Schopenhauer, was no moral force but merely a mechanism for preserving law and order so as to ensure the safety of its citizens and their property. Nevertheless, he was more than happy to take advantage of the educational

Friedrich Bury,
a chalk sketch of
Johann Gottlieb
Fichte, *c*. 1800.

opportunities provided by the distinguished professors who had
been drawn to Berlin by the creation of the new university. Just as
he had at Göttingen, Schopenhauer enrolled in a very wide range
of classes. This is Helen Zimmern's summary:

> That first winter he attended Fichte's lectures on Philosophy,
> besides classes on Experimental Chemistry, Magnetism and
> Electricity, Ornithology, Amphibiology, Ichthyology, Domestic
> Animals, and Norse Poetry. Between the years 1812–13 he heard
> Schleiermacher read on the 'History of Philosophy since the
> time of Christ', Wolf on the 'Clouds' of Aristophanes, the 'Satires'
> of Horace, and Greek Antiquities, still continuing his natural
> history studies of Physics, Astronomy, General Physiology,
> Zoology and Geography.[4]

But whereas at Göttingen the extraordinary energy and perseverance he brought to his studies were initially fuelled by his need to catch up on what was missing in his education, in Berlin his motivation came more from his desire to assimilate everything worth knowing. By now he was aware that his commitment to philosophy required that he develop a system of thought. In this respect, Schopenhauer was no different from the other philosophers of his time, in that they aimed to produce a philosophical system that would encompass 'the totality of experience' or 'the totality of things' (*MR* I, p. 21). Within a year of his arrival in Berlin he was sketching an outline of what he labelled 'A Little System', and by 1813 he noted that he felt within him a work of philosophy, growing 'by degrees like a child in the womb' (*MR* I, p. 59). This philosophy would live, he believed, only if it emerged as an organic whole of which all the constituent parts were mutually reinforcing. As such, it would differ from the ideal of modern philosophers: to present a system of thought as a deduction from first principles. He elaborates on this contrast in the Preface to *The World as Will and Representation,* claiming that his work is an expression of 'a single thought' (*WWR* I, p. xii).

Schopenhauer characterized one aspect of his distinctive capacity as a philosopher by saying that the perplexity that, according to Plato, is the source of philosophy was for him 'a perplexity concerning the world', whereas that of the bogus philosopher is 'a perplexity concerning some existing system' (*MR* I, p. 81). Thus, for Schopenhauer, the problems that motivate genuine philosophical reflection do not arise from reading books or hearing lectures – they are not problems stemming from concepts – but from observation of the world, in particular the presence of death together with 'the suffering and misery of life . . . If our life were without end and free from pain, it would possibly not occur to anyone to ask why the world exists, and why it does so in precisely this way' (*WWR* II, p. 161). It was because Schopenhauer had such a keen sense of these motivating

questions that the philosophy he felt growing within him was to be
– what Nietzsche recognized as inherent in all great philosophy –
'ethics and metaphysics *in one*, for hitherto these were just as falsely
separated as was man into body and soul' (*MR* I, p. 59). The aim of
his philosophy was not to lose sight of our experience of the world
in a blaze of abstract theory, but to explain it thoroughly. Hence it
was of concern to Schopenhauer that his philosophy should not
just be consistent with the known facts of the world as discovered by
science, but provide a deeper understanding of them. Throughout
his life Schopenhauer maintained the habit he had formed as a
student of keeping abreast with the latest developments in science,
even in some cases maintaining contact with his Berlin teachers, such
as the physicist Paul Erman and the zoologist Martin Lichtenstein.[5]
And he made this grasp of the sciences explicit when, in 1836, he
published his book *On the Will in Nature* in order, as the subtitle
makes clear, to discuss *the Corroborations from the Empirical Sciences
that the Author's Philosophy has Received since its first Appearance.*
He continued to revise the book until his death in 1860. By then,
his library contained almost 200 works in the natural sciences in
various languages.[6]

In his first semester at Berlin Schopenhauer attended the all-
important lectures in philosophy by Fichte himself, beginning with
introductory lectures on the study of philosophy together with
'On the Facts of Consciousness'. He made copious notes on these
lectures, as indeed he did on most of the other lectures he attended,
some of which were written from memory afterwards. The notes
are studded with his own observations, comments and criticisms,
and points of philosophical agreement and disagreement. Yet in the
very first lecture he recorded a problem of another kind – obscurity
and inadequate explanation (*MR* II, p. 18). At first Schopenhauer
put this down to his own lapses in concentration, due, in part, to
Fichte's method of delivery. Fichte prided himself on talking his way
through the issues with his class rather than reading his lectures to

them, as was the general custom. Schopenhauer slowly came around to the belief that his difficulties in understanding were Fichte's fault and did not stem from his own inattention or lack of intelligence. Increasing impatience triggered his irritation: 'he has explained absolutely nothing at all'; 'I do not know what this means.' And then, in the eleventh lecture, he snapped.

> In this lecture . . . he has said things which have wrung from me the wish to be allowed to put a pistol to his chest and then to say: Now you must die without mercy, but for the sake of your poor soul say whether with this jumble of words you have a clear conception of anything or have merely made fools of us. (*MR* II, p. 43)

Some lectures later, Schopenhauer noted despondently that he had written nothing down for eight days. Disillusioned, he fashioned a trademark witticism: Fichte's lecture title, 'On the Doctrine of Science [*Wissenschaftslehre*]', was best understood as the 'emptiness of science [*Wissenschaftsleere*]' (*MR* II, p. 31).

The ostensible reason for Schopenhauer's disillusion was Fichte's penchant for convoluted and paradoxical forms of expression. In this respect, Fichte was not much different from his peers in the forefront of early nineteenth-century philosophy. Schopenhauer would, in the course of his own writing career, pour scorn and contempt on what he regarded as these defamers of the German language. But there were deeper reasons for Schopenhauer's irritation with Fichte. For one thing, Fichte liked to present himself not only as the one true heir to Kant, but the pre-eminent philosophical authority of the era. This was bound to grate on the stubborn self-belief of Schopenhauer, who felt that he had a philosophy within him which would supersede all others. Moreover, since the late summer of 1811, Schopenhauer had been reading Kant intensively and, notwith-standing the difficulties he found in Kant – for he was never an

Immanuel Kant (aged 67) in an engraving of 1791 by Gottlieb Döbler, after an anonymous oil painting.

uncritical admirer of the critical philosophy – he had come to recognize the greatness of Kant's achievement. But Fichte, Schopenhauer believed, did not properly grasp Kant's views any more than Schelling and Hegel did. Basing his own system on that of Kant, Schopenhauer eventually came to see himself as Kant's true philosophical heir.

In order to account for the a priori truths of science and mathematics, expressed in such judgements as 'Every event has a cause', 'The shortest distance between two points is a straight line', and '2 + 2 = 4', Kant argued that it was necessary to accept that the mind or human consciousness plays a role in the formation of objective knowledge, knowledge of objects. This is the core of Kant's so-called Copernican Revolution in philosophy: whereas philosophers prior to Kant had 'assumed that all our knowledge must conform to objects', Kant proposed that 'objects must conform to our knowledge'.[7] This strategy has the weakness that it seems to undermine the reality of objects, treating them as mind-dependent and so rendering all knowledge subjective rather than genuinely objective. Kant believed he could avoid this weakness by drawing a distinction between objects as we know them in experience (*phenomena*) and as they are independently of our experience of them (*noumena*). Objects as we know them in experience are in space and time and interact causally with one another. Kant maintains that these structural features of objects as we know them are due to the ways in which our minds perceive and categorize objects: in effect, our minds supply the fundamental forms that shape the crude matter provided by objects as they are independently of our experience. Since, as Kant maintained, experience is necessary for knowledge of objects, it follows that we can never know objects as they are independent of our experience of them. Noumena are thus unknowable: yet Kant never denies their reality. The thing-in-itself (*ding an sich*) is 'indeed real *per se*, but . . . not known by us'.[8] To distinguish his position from idealism, the view that all objects are mind-dependent, and realism, the view that all objects are independent of mind, Kant coined the term Transcendental Idealism.

The prominent post-Kantian idealists such as Fichte, Schelling and Hegel were united in their opposition to Kant's Transcendental Idealism. Schopenhauer, however, was obdurate in its defence. Indeed, by the time of writing *The World as Will and Representation*, he went so far as to assert in the Appendix on Kant's philosophy that 'Kant's greatest merit is the distinction of the phenomenon from the thing-in-itself' (I, p. 417). Nevertheless, Schopenhauer was always acutely conscious of difficulties in Kant's account of the thing-in-itself, difficulties that had been raised by his teacher, Schulze, and that had been taken further by Fichte himself in his *Wissenschaftslehre* of 1794. Fichte argued that Kant's commitment to both the active, constructive capacity of consciousness and the givenness of reality, the thing-in-itself, generated an instability that could be resolved only by rejecting one or the other. But to reject the constructive capacity of consciousness in favour of the thing-in-itself would, he maintained, ultimately lead to materialism and determinism, thereby undermining Kant's own theory of freedom and moral action as presented in the *Critique of Practical Reason* (1788). Fichte therefore proposed to jettison the Kantian thing-in-itself, aiming for a 'complete deduction of all experience from the possibility of self consciousness'.[9] That is to say, according to Fichte, it is possible to account for the objective world of experience entirely in terms of the a priori constructive operations of the subjective consciousness without reference to a mind-independent reality. In his notes on Fichte's lectures Schopenhauer wrote that 'Kant's great truth' had been replaced by Fichte's 'raving nonsense . . . the concoction of his own brain' (*MR* II, p. 134). Later, he scornfully characterized Fichte's explanation of the objective in terms of the subjective as like trying to make 'the non-ego result from the ego as the web from the spider' (*WWR* I, p. 33). To reduce the object to the subject, he argued, was no less mistaken than Schelling's reduction of the subject to the object; for, as he put it in his notes on Schelling, 'object and subject are conceivable only as the one in reference to the other' (*MR* II, p. 381; cf. *WWR* I, p. 5). It is Schopenhauer's defence of the necessity of this Kantian duality, together with his subsequent resolution of the problems posed by the notion of the thing-in-itself, that justifies Schopenhauer's conviction that he alone among the post-Kantian generation was a genuine Kantian.

At the same time that he was grappling with Kant's critical philosophy and its successors, Schopenhauer was entering remarks in his private notebook, as distinct from his lecture notebooks, that show him groping his way towards a conception of the inner life which he was to name as the better or higher consciousness (*MR* I, pp. 14, 23, 27, 33). With this idea Schopenhauer brought together his earliest pre-philosophical reflections, based on his intense adolescent experiences of aesthetic rapture and his religious, romantic yearning to escape from the turmoil and pain of daily life, with his continuously evolving explorations of moral, aesthetic and religious concepts such as freedom, happiness, virtue, genius and saintliness. Schopenhauer made much use of this idea of the better consciousness during his time in Berlin as he devoted more effort to producing his own philosophical system. Yet the concept of the better consciousness is not mentioned in his PhD dissertation, completed in 1813. And it does not figure in the philosophy that Schopenhauer was to elaborate in *The World as Will and Representation.* Nevertheless, it was the unifying role provided by this idea that ultimately led to Schopenhauer's discovery of the deep structure of that mature philosophy.

The presiding inspiration behind the conception of the better consciousness was not Kant, but Plato: in particular, Plato's separation of the mundane spatio-temporal world of ever-changing sights and sounds from the timeless reality of the world of Ideas, the divine home of beauty, goodness and truth. Plato's duality of worlds is mirrored by Schopenhauer's characterization of human consciousness as a mixture of eternity and temporality. Everyday life, dominated by interaction with material things, with people and places,
is mired in temporality. When we rise above such everydayness in moments of aesthetic enjoyment of nature and art, or in mystical contemplation of life and the world, we experience the stirrings of the better consciousness and are in touch with timeless realities, the Platonic Ideas themselves (*MR* I, pp. 43, 49–50). However, the realm of the better consciousness is not just a means of escape from

temporality, which is by itself nothing but a realm of chance, error, wickedness and violence: it is also a source of what is good and valuable in human existence. For ordinary human wickedness can be opposed by love and human feeling, which are expressions of the better consciousness (*MR* I, p. 55). Hence it is the better consciousness that makes true virtue and saintliness possible.

This account of moral motivation brought Schopenhauer into conflict with Kant's theory as elaborated in his *Groundwork of the Metaphysics of Morals* (1785) and *Critique of Practical Reason* (1788). There Kant argued that moral conduct is action undertaken in accordance with universal maxims consistent with the Categorical Imperative, a principle of a priori rationality and the supreme principle of morality. Schopenhauer fiercely opposed Kant's attempt to ground morality in reason.

> But to deduce from reason (*Vernunft*) the moral element in conduct is blasphemy. In this element there is expressed *the better consciousness* which lies *far above all reason*, expresses itself in conduct as holiness, and is the true salvation of the world. This same consciousness expresses itself in art as genius, as a consolation for the temporal and earthly state. (*MR* I, p. 47)

In spite of his immense admiration for what Kant achieved in the philosophy of theoretical reason, Schopenhauer was a consistent and caustic critic of Kant's philosophy of practical reason, culminating in 1839 with the publication of *On the Basis of Morality*, in which he declared that his own view of the foundation of morality was 'diametrically opposed to Kant's' (*BM/TFP*, pp. 47/122).

Not only did Schopenhauer think that the better consciousness was above all reason, he also claimed that the better consciousness lifts us into a world where there is no longer personality, causality nor subject and object (*MR* I, p. 44). And since, as Schopenhauer acknowledges, personality and causality are necessary characteristics of God, it follows that the world of the better consciousness cannot be understood by reference to the concept of God. Nevertheless, Schopenhauer concedes that the expression 'God' might be employed *symbolically* to name the better consciousness, though to do so would court confusion. Here Schopenhauer touches on an issue that was to be crucial for his mature philosophy: the relation of religion to philosophy. The position he took, that religion is independent of philosophy, put him at odds with most contemporary philosophers and indeed with the political authorities of the day. It was an issue he confronted personally for the first time while attending lectures on the 'History of Philosophy during the Period of Christianity' given by Schleiermacher in 1812.

Friedrich Schleiermacher (1768–1834) was a leading Protestant theologian whose work on the interpretation of the New Testament, as well as his philosophical reflection on the nature of interpretation, laid the foundations for the development of hermeneutics. As a prominent figure in the establishment of the new University of Berlin, he defended the orthodox view that religion and philosophy have in common the knowledge of God. Schopenhauer's notes on Schleiermacher's lectures record his objections sentence by sentence. To Schleiermacher's assertion that the philosopher and the religious person mutually acknowledge that their objects of knowledge are identical, Schopenhauer wrote that philosophy is 'something much loftier than any possible religion . . . which it must grasp and see through'. To Schleiermacher's claim that 'transcendental philosophy ends in the knowledge of God', Schopenhauer responded, 'This is a shameless obtrusion of the concept of God.' And when Schleiermacher pronounced,

Philosophy and religion cannot exist without one another; no one can be a philosopher without being religious. Conversely, the religious person must at least make the the problem of philosophy his own,

Schopenhauer replied,

> No one who is religious attains to philosophy; he does not need
> it. No one who really philosophizes is religious; he walks with-
> out leading-strings, perilously but free. (*MR* II, pp. 241–3)

The genuine philosopher, as opposed to the pseudo-philoso-
pher, does not assume the concept of God, as the religious person
does; rather, he questions it by considering its legitimacy and
intelligibility. To make religious truth a condition of the outcome
of philosophical enquiry would simply prevent the philosopher
from performing his task as a philosopher. That the philosophers
of the German universities were thus shackled in their pursuit
of truth by their religious obligations was persistently asserted
by Schopenhauer.

Throughout 1812 and the opening months of 1813, while
Schopenhauer was descending ever further into the depths of
philosophy, the political situation of Prussia, and of Berlin in
particular, grew steadily darker and more dangerous. In the spring
of 1812 the state provided 20,000 men for Napoleon's *Grande Armée*,
billeted in Berlin en route to the invasion of Russia, which had
defected from the anti-British alliance. But the Prussian army was
not involved in the advance to Moscow or the subsequent catastrophic retreat through the Russian steppes in December 1812.
When the Prussian General decided, in defiance of King Frederick
William, to conclude the Convention of Tauroggen with Russia at
the end of December, plans were soon implemented for mobiliza-
tion in support of an uprising against Napoleon. Meanwhile,
the battered remnants of the French army limped into Berlin in
January 1813. None of this impinged directly upon Schopenhauer
until war was declared in March, following the King's proclamation
calling upon individuals to 'fight and conquer unless we wish to
cease to be Prussians and Germans'. Classes at the university were

closed and most of the students rallied to the cause. Schopenhauer did not, maintaining 'my fatherland is greater than Germany' (*GB*, p. 643), although he did contribute financially to equipping a friend who had volunteered. Fichte and Schleiermacher, on the other hand, saw no incompatibility between their commitment to philosophy and patriotism. Schleiermacher led the church service that inaugurated the official opening of the war on 28 March. Fichte bravely volunteered at the age of 51 to be a field preacher at Prussian headquarters. This request was refused but Fichte died soon after, in January 1814, when he contracted typhus from his wife, who had been tending the sick and wounded at a military hospital.

After the Battle of Lützen in early May, with the threat of an attack on Berlin from Napoleon's troops continuing to escalate, and 'haunted by the fear of being pressed into military service' (*MR* IV, p. 507), Schopenhauer decided that he needed to find a safer, more peaceful location in which to continue his philosophical work. He set off towards Dresden but, in the confusion typical of the times, found himself compelled in one small village to act as an interpreter between the mayor and the French soldiers there. On reaching Dresden he felt no safer than he had in Berlin, and set off again, this time for Weimar and his mother's apartments. It was unlikely, in view of their previous difficulties in living together, that this would prove anything other than a temporary halt in his travels. In the event, the domestic circumstances were even more unsatisfactory than hitherto. To Schopenhauer's surprise, he discovered that sharing the accommodation was Privy Councillor Georg Friedrich Conrad Müller, who had become Johanna's close companion since they met in 1810. Goethe's wife, Christiane, even feared they would marry. Not surprisingly, Schopenhauer was aghast, not least for the affront, as he saw it, to the memory of his father. Within a month, he travelled 40 kilometres further south to the village of Rudolstadt, where he took an upper room at a small inn from June to November 1813. Here, in comparative isolation from the noisy, warlike world, he was able to

An anonymous, undated portrait of Georg Friedrich (Müller) von Gerstenbergk.

settle himself to compose his PhD dissertation. The 'inexpressible charms of the region' – the mountains and woods of Thuringia – played their role in allowing him to overcome familiar doubts and anxieties. As he later put it in his *curriculum vitae*,

> I was happy in that valley, encircled by wooded mountains . . . within the deepest solitude, distracted and diverted by nothing, uninterrupted, I applied myself to the most remote problems and investigations. (*GB* p. 654)

While the charms of wooded mountains may have stirred the better consciousness in Schopenhauer, he chose not to make the better consciousness the subject of his dissertation. There were just too many unresolved problems about the notion that would have interfered with his aim of obtaining his university qualification. For a similar reason, he avoided direct confrontation with what he called in the dissertation Kant's 'notorious thing-in-itself'.[10] Instead, he concentrated his attention on the realm of the empirical consciousness, as conceived in Kant's critical philosophy, thereby establishing his credentials as a Kantian at the same time as pointing out and correcting what he took to be Kant's mistakes. That is to say, in the terms of his finished system, the dissertation deals with the world as representation rather than with the world as will. Indeed, in the preface to the first edition of *The World as Will and Representation*, he presented his dissertation as an essential introduction to it, maintaining that it would be impossible to understand his philosophy without a grasp of the arguments of his dissertation. When Schopenhauer came to prepare a second edition of his dissertation for publication in 1837, he completely revised and expanded the text in accordance with the views of his mature philosophy; the result is that the version of *The Fourfold Root* that is now most often read provides a misleading impression of Schopenhauer's conception of the dissertation which he wrote among the wooded mountains of Thuringia. The style and tone of the second edition are also radically different. Not surprisingly, the Schopenhauer of 1813 writes with the studied conscientiousness and sober academic manner befitting a student submitting work for a university degree, whereas the Schopenhauer of 1837, confident in his intellectual and philosophical powers, is eager to display his prodigious learning and to trumpet the merits of his philosophy while neglecting no opportunity to abuse the eminent German philosophers of the era.

The title Schopenhauer chose for his dissertation, *Über die vierfache Wurzel des Satzes vom zureichenden Grunde* (usually translated as *On the Fourfold Root of the Principle of Sufficient Reason*), indicates that the topic of his work is the so-called principle of sufficient reason: that nothing is without a reason why it is rather than is not (*EFR*, §5, p. 4).[11] Schopenhauer sees this principle as the basis of science or empirical knowledge, for it underlies our quest for explanations of events and states of affairs in the world around us. When we assume that there are reasons why things are as they are, causes that explain why changes have occurred, grounds which show why judgements are true, we take the principle for granted. But although philosophers throughout history, even as far back as Plato and Aristotle, have acknowledged the importance of such a principle of reasoning, Schopenhauer contends that they have not been sufficiently clear about the different forms explanation can take, the different roots of the principle in understanding the world. Hence Schopenhauer's aim in his dissertation is to establish the status of the principle and display its applications in order to achieve the 'clarity and lucidity' that is the proper aim of philosophy. And in a memorable image he notes that philosophy should 'resemble not a turbid, impetuous torrent, bur rather a Swiss lake which by its calm combines great depth with great clearness, the depth revealing itself precisely through the clearness' (*FR*, §3, p. 4).

Schopenhauer distinguishes four different forms of explanation, four forms that the principle of sufficient reason takes, according to the four kinds of objects that can be identified; and corresponding to these four forms of explanation are the disciplines of physical science, logic, mathematics and ethics. First, there are objects in space and time whose interactions are understood within the physical sciences by reference to the causal principle that every event has a cause. Second, there are concepts, the constituents of judgements. As a matter of logic, if they are to express knowledge and count as truths, these must be sufficiently grounded in some-thing outside themselves. Third, space and time, distinct from objects in space and time, provide the contents of mathematical explanations: the infinite parts of space, or points, and the infinite parts of time, or moments, are related to and dependent upon one another, and these relationships are expressed in the truths of geometry and arithmetic respectively. Fourth, ethics is concerned with individual subjects of willing whose movements are explained in terms of motives, for motives cause acts of will or actions in the same way as events in the physical world are caused; but since human subjects are generally aware of their own motives, Schopenhauer characterizes them in the second edition as 'causes seen from within' (*FR*, §43, p. 214). Failure to observe these four forms of explanation, Schopenhauer argues, led previous philosophers into error; and in the conclusion of the dissertation he illustrates Kant's confusion in speaking of the thing-in-itself sometimes as the reason or ground of phenomenal reality and sometimes as its cause (*EFR*, §59, p. 68).

Even though Schopenhauer was not at the time of writing his dissertation prepared to take on the problem of the Kantian thing-in-itself, throughout the dissertation he repeatedly articulates his own position by spelling out how he agrees with and differs from Kant on the topics he addresses. He was in fundamental agreement with Kant over the a priori character of the principle of sufficient reason: the principle is not susceptible to proof for the simple reason that it is presupposed in any argument or proof (*EFR* §13, pp. 9–10; *FR*, §14, pp. 32–3). Furthermore, he follows Kant in accepting that space and time, and causality, are a priori forms, of sensibility and understanding respectively. Schopenhauer takes this to imply idealism: objects are mind-dependent. 'To be object for a subject and to be representation is to be one and the same thing. All representations are objects for a subject, all objects for a subject are representations' (*EFR* §16, pp. 13; *FR*, §16, pp. 41–2). Schopenhauer dispenses with Kant's a priori categories, since all interrelations between representations are given through the principle of sufficient reason. This leads to a drastic simplification of the apparatus of Kant's transcendental psychology. Furthermore, Schopenhauer develops a theory of

Olaf Gulbrannson's cartoon of Kant looking over Schopenhauer's shoulder.

perception that is wholly different from Kant's. For Kant perception involves judgement, the application of concepts, whereas Schopenhauer denies that concepts enter into perception. For Schopenhauer concepts are abstractions from perception, what he calls representations of representations, and are linked to the creation of language, something beyond the capacity of non-human animals. Perception, Schopenhauer argues, involves an 'inference of the understanding' that does not rely on concepts. It is thus common to human and non-human animal perception. Schopenhauer's concern with consciousness rather than intellectual judgement enables him to recognize the continuity between the human and the non-human subject: even if animals lack concepts they nonetheless perceive and respond to their environments in a manner similar to people.

Schopenhauer devoted the summer of 1813, from mid-June to mid-September, to intensive work on his dissertation, taking time out in his usual manner to go for long walks in the hills and play his flute. He had intended to submit the dissertation to the University of Berlin, but the Franco–Prussian war had by now spread south through Germany and it was no longer safe to send such a precious manuscript on the road from Rudolstadt to Berlin. Rather than waiting for the end of hostilities, he turned to the nearby University of Jena and contacted the Dean of the Faculty of Philosophy with a view to submitting his dissertation for a degree *in absentia.* It is likely that Schopenhauer received favourable treatment from the Dean, who knew him to be the son of Johanna Schopenhauer, the author and friend of Goethe, who was himself the university's ducal plenipotentiary. On 24 September, within days of paying his graduating fee, Schopenhauer sent in the manuscript of his dissertation together with a letter, uncharacteristically modest in tone, expressing concern over possible weaknesses in his work and at the same time describing his educational history and the circumstances that led him to submit it to Jena rather than Berlin. Despite his formal display of diffidence, Schopenhauer was confident enough of success to arrange publication at his own expense with a publisher in Rudolstadt. With remarkable swiftness, Schopenhauer's degree was granted *magna cum laude* on 2 October; by 5 October he had received his diploma of Doctor of Philosophy.

It was in October, while he was waiting for the publication of his dissertation, that the tranquillity of Rudolstadt was interrupted by the war. On 18 October Napoleon's army was defeated at the battle of Leipzig by a coalition of Prussian, Austrian and Russian forces, with casualties of over 100,000 dead or injured. Survivors began to appear in the region of Rudolstadt, disturbing the calm that Schopenhauer had relished. It was time for him to move on. On 5 November he found himself once again in Weimar, though no longer a struggling student but a Doctor of Philosophy confident of his intellectual destiny.

4

The Great Work

Schopenhauer's task after completing his dissertation was to give birth to the philosophical system that had been growing within him for a couple of years. Yet he had no idea on returning to Weimar that there he would encounter the ideas of ancient Indian religion which were to be a seminal influence on his own thinking. Together with what he had already absorbed from Plato and Kant, they radically transformed his conception of the relation of the better consciousness to the empirical consciousness, enabling him both to resolve the problems he had been grappling with and to articulate a distinctively personal, wholly original, philosophy. As he put it in 1816, 'I do not believe that my theory could have come about before the *Upanishads*, Plato, and Kant could cast their rays simultaneously into the mind of one man' (*MR* I, p. 467). It would take another five years of concentrated work before Schopenhauer could bring those rays together in his magnum opus.

Immediately on his return to Weimar in November 1813, however, he found himself plunged into a domestic maelstrom which would leave permanent scars in his life. Conscious of his mother's previous admonition against their living together and of the continued presence in her home of Privy Councillor Müller – who in 1815 adopted the title of von Gerstenbergk – Schopenhauer settled himself in a local inn. But then, unexpectedly, and with tears, Johanna begged him to take up residence with his family. In a later letter, justifying her request, she explained that his doing so would, she hoped, prevent Schopenhauer from getting any 'wrong ideas' about her domestic arrangements.[1] By this she meant that Schopenhauer would see for himself that there was no impropriety in her relationship with Gerstenbergk and that he need not worry that she had intentions of marrying the Privy Councillor. Johanna understood her son's temperament too well. He was suspicious of his mother's friendship; he did fear she might marry Gerstenbergk. But Johanna's plea for Schopenhauer to join her household was a catastrophic mistake for the family.

With a university doctorate and a published work of philosophy to his credit, Schopenhauer could take pride in these public demonstrations of what he had achieved since he set out for Berlin two years before. Johanna had not been idle either. She had written her second book, a volume of reminiscences of her travels in the years 1803–5. It was published in the winter of 1813 – coincidentally, by the same publishing house that had brought out Schopenhauer's dissertation – and was a considerable success, establishing her identity as a talented author. Johanna subsequently published another volume of travel memoirs, then short stories and eventually novels, one after another. At the beginning of the 1830s, her collected works numbered 24 volumes and her fame eclipsed that of her son's during and beyond her own lifetime. Schopenhauer, not surprisingly, regarded Johanna's publications as light entertainment compared to the weighty significance of his philosophical work. He later reported a memorable occasion of mutual slanging. Referring to the title of his dissertation, *The Fourfold Root*, Johanna teasingly remarked that the book must have been intended for pharmacists. To this Schopenhauer brutally responded, 'It will still be read when hardly a copy of your writings can be found in a junk room.' 'And', Johanna hit back, 'the entire printing of yours will have yet to be sold' (G, p. 17). There was truth in both observations. While Schopenhauer's works are now read even though Johanna's name is virtually forgotten, it was not until the end of Schopenhauer's life that editions of his works actually sold out.

The antagonism between mother and son is evident in this duel of caustic wit, which took place soon after Schopenhauer's return. The tensions were to fester in the ensuing months until the inevitable, final explosive confrontation came in May 1814. Their differences in temperament and outlook and the accumulated grievances and resentment that made their living together uncomfortable were exacerbated by Gerstenbergk's place in the household. The ambitious civil servant from Ronneburg, where he and Johanna had met in 1810, probably did rely on Johanna's friendship with Goethe as a means of entry into Weimar society, but there is little doubt that their relationship was genuine. They shared an enthusiasm for literature and art, encouraged and supported one another's literary projects – Johanna included some of his poems in her novel *Gabriele* (1819) – and were company for one another in their numerous social engagements. Though fourteen years younger than Johanna, Gerstenbergk took over the role previously played by Fernow as her confidant and advisor, looked after her household in her absence and offered financial support when she lost most of her investments in 1819.

Schopenhauer found Gerstenbergk intolerable: he not only regarded him personally as undistinguished and uninteresting, but resented the way in which Gerstenbergk had insinuated himself into the position in the household that Schopenhauer, as the son and heir of Heinrich Floris Schopenhauer, would naturally occupy. Hamlet-like, Schopenhauer directed his venom at his mother's friend, leading to bitter quarrels between the two men. Johanna stood up for Gerstenbergk but attempted to ameliorate matters by arranging for him to take his meals elsewhere. Two further personalities compounded the conflict. First, there was a student friend of Schopenhauer's from Berlin, Josef Gans, who joined the household at Schopenhauer's expense in January 1814, and who

Alexander von Ungern-Sternberg's sketch of Adele Schopenhauer (aged 44), 1841.

tended to side with his benefactor. And there was Adele, Schopenhauer's sister, now at the vulnerable age of sixteen, who was dismayed by the hostility of the clashes between her mother and brother. Denied a formal education, as was typical for girls of her class at the time, Adele was nonetheless an intelligent and gifted young woman who later achieved modest fame writing poems, stories and novels. If, like Schopenhauer, she owed her literary talents to her mother, then, like her brother, she owed to her father something of her melancholic disposition.

Adele dreaded the prospect of life as a spinster, yet her unprepossessing appearance, coupled with her freethinking intelligence, did not attract suitors. Johanna once suggested to her that she should

Gerhard von Kügelgen, *Johanna Schopenhauer* (aged 48) 1814, oil on canvas.

think of marrying Gerstenbergk, but this only compounded her already conflicted loyalties towards her mother and brother.[2]

By April 1814 Johanna could no longer stand the daily moods, quarrels and stony silences. She explained to Schopenhauer – in a letter taken by the maid from one room to another! – her wish that he should leave and take his friend Gans with him. Schopenhauer's offer to increase the rent he paid for his rooms led to further financial wrangling. An unusually heated altercation between mother and son on 16 May resulted in Schopenhauer violently slamming the door behind him as he left the room. They were never to meet again. The following day Johanna wrote him a letter in which she deployed her literary skill to convey the depth of her distress,

announcing that the door he had slammed so noisily 'is closed
forever between you and me'. She told him she could not see him
again out of fear for her health – another quarrel could bring on
a stroke that might be fatal; her mother's heart felt every blow from
a once loved hand. Blaming Schopenhauer's mistrust of her life,
contempt for her sex, his greed and his moods for the rift between
them, she reminded him of his father's request before his death
that he should honour his mother: 'what would he say if he saw
your behaviour?' The letter ended dramatically with the declaration,
'My duty towards you is at an end, go your way, I have nothing more
to do with you . . . You have hurt me too much. Live and be as happy
as you can be.'[3] Schopenhauer soon left Weimar for Dresden.[4]
Although freeing him from the emotional imbroglio of the
Weimar household, his mother's rejection inflicted a wound
which never healed.

Remarkably, the upheavals in his home life did not seriously
impinge on Schopenhauer's intellectual progress during the
winter of 1813–14. Everything, he wrote in April, was peripheral
and subordinate to his philosophical studies, his 'better and real life'
(*GB*, p. 10). Two meetings in Johanna's salon had been momentous:
the first with Goethe, the second with Frederich Majer. It was the
second rather than the first that proved to be of lasting significance
for his philosophy.

From the time that Schopenhauer had first attended Johanna's
social events, Goethe had shown little interest in him. But on his
return to Weimar as a Doctor of Philosophy, Goethe suddenly rose
from his seat, walked over to him, shook his hand and expressed his
praise for the dissertation, which he considered highly significant
(*G*, p. 26). Schopenhauer had sent Goethe a copy of his dissertation
and was thrilled to hear him give public utterance to his good
opinion of it.[5] He was invited to call on Goethe at his house on the
Frauenplan. After that first private meeting, Schopenhauer wrote
ecstatically to Professor Wolf in Berlin informing him that his friend,

'our great Goethe', was sociable, obliging and friendly: 'praised be his name for ever' (*GB*, p. 7). Their meetings occurred regularly throughout the winter months. However, Goethe's motives for continuing discussion with Schopenhauer were not entirely disinterested, for the primary subject of conversation was not Schopenhauer's philosophy but rather Goethe's theory of colour. The two volumes of his *Zur Farbenlehre* were published in 1810 and, to Goethe's surprise and immense disappointment, his long-pondered reflections on the nature of light and colour were poorly received by scientists and the general public. In Schopenhauer, Goethe believed he had found a like-minded thinker who would support him in his campaign to overthrow the Newtonian theory of colour. He had misjudged Schopenhauer's character. Though Schopenhauer embarked enthusiastically on a study of the topic, he was not a man to play second fiddle to anyone. He set himself to produce a theory of colour to replace both Newton's and Goethe's, in short, to achieve what he was later to describe in a letter to Goethe as the 'first true theory of colour, the first in the whole history of science' (*GB*, p. 20).

Schopenhauer did not seriously dispute Goethe's data, for Goethe had taken him through some of the crucial experiments and even lent him some of his optical apparatus; and he accepted Goethe's critique of Newton, agreeing that colours could not be understood in terms of the wavelengths of light rays independent of vision. By taking visual experience into account, Goethe represented colours as a kind of shadow arising from the interplay of the presence and absence of light, the blending of lightness (or white) and dark-ness (or black). But he regarded light and dark to be primary phenomena (*Urphänomen*), incapable of further explanation, a position that is incompatible with Schopenhauer's idealism. Schopenhauer reported to a friend in later life that Goethe was so totally a realist that he completely refused to consider that objects themselves exist only insofar as they are represented by the knowing subject. 'He once said to me, staring at me with his Jupiter eyes, "Is the light there only when you see it? No, you would not exist if the light did not see you"' (*g*, p. 31).[6] In line with the account he had given of perception in his dissertation, Schopenhauer regarded the essence of colour as 'thoroughly subjective' (*vc*, p. 8), entirely dependent on the seeing eye. Thus, for Schopenhauer, colours are modifications of the eye. By assigning the numerical values of zero to retinal inactivity (black) and one to full retinal activity (white), Schopenhauer was able to maintain that

> the difference between colours is the result of the difference between the qualitative halves into which this [retinal] activity can be separated, and of their ratio to one another. These halves can be *equal* only once, and they then exhibit true red and perfect green. They can be *unequal* in innumerable ratios and hence the number of possible colours is infinite. (*vc*, pp. 31–2)

However, Schopenhauer conceded that these retinal ratios were 'hypothetical' – that is, entirely speculative – since they could not be 'proved for the present' (*vc*, p. 30).[7]

The manuscript of *On Vision and Colours* was composed in a few weeks a year or so after Schopenhauer arrived in Dresden and it was immediately sent to Goethe. It became his second publication when it appeared in print at Easter 1816. The delay in publication was due, as Schopenhauer explained in the Preface to the second edition of 1854, to Goethe's tardiness in returning the manuscript (*vc*, p. 1). When Schopenhauer sent the manuscript in July 1815, he had hoped that Goethe would at least acknowledge its superiority to his own, if not admit to total acceptance of the new theory. But Goethe was wise to the young man's arrogance and ambition. He had already composed some verse with Schopenhauer in mind around the time they had discontinued their discussions. 'I would like to bear the teacher's burdens still longer, /If only the pupils did not at once become teachers.'[8] In their ensuing correspondence, Goethe showed much patience, generosity and good humour in the face of Schopenhauer's increasingly assertive demands for him to state his opinion of the new theory. When he could endure Goethe's evasiveness no longer, Schopenhauer asked for his manuscript to be returned and then had it published without Goethe's blessing. Schopenhauer's frustration and disappointment in no way lessened his esteem for Goethe, whom he placed alongside Kant as the two greatest men of the German nation (*PP* II, p. 198). All his life he championed Goethe's contribution to colour theory, maintaining its superiority to Newton's for its 'systematic presentation of the facts' (*VC*, p. 6; cf. p. 50). Ironically, Schopenhauer's theory suffered the same neglect and ignominy as Goethe's. Yet whereas Goethe's theory of colour was the work of twenty years and was regarded by him as the summit of his achievement, Schopenhauer thought of his own work on colour as a 'sideline' to the very different theories developed during his four years in Dresden (*GB*, p. 22; cf. *MR* IV, p. 392).

Schopenhauer made his home in Dresden from mid-1814 to late 1818. He chose Dresden as the birthplace of his philosophy out of admiration for the beautiful city, which he had visited on numerous occasions in his youth, though before moving there he sought assurances that it had sufficiently recovered from the terrible events of the previous year: it had suffered immense damage during the French victory in the battle for Dresden and the subsequent siege by the coalition forces. From the late eighteenth century and throughout the nineteenth, Dresden was a major centre of art, architecture and music, with a magnificent collection of paintings housed in a wing of the Zwinger Palace and a well-established opera house (which in 1816 came under the directorship of Carl Maria von Weber). It was also the home of one of the world's oldest orchestras, the celebrated Royal Saxony Orchestra, founded in 1548. All of these were features attractive to Schopenhauer, as was a large library, a pleasing climate and a thriving artistic community. There were many writers of national reputation living in Dresden, like Friedrich Schulze (who wrote under the pseudonym of Friedrich Laun), Theodor Hell and Friedrich Kind.[9] Dresden was also home to Germany's greatest Romantic artist, Caspar David Friedrich, whose landscape paintings exemplify the mystical contemplation of nature. Schopenhauer might well have encountered him, sketchbook in hand, on his walks in the hills to the east of the city.

Though Schopenhauer's concentration on his work required solitude, he did not shun society as he had while writing his dissertation. He was a regular visitor to the theatre and opera, where it was the Italian operas that appealed to him rather than the German operas favoured by Weber. Rossini's operas were his favourite and he had flute arrangements of them all (*G*, p. 221). Schopenhauer also frequented the Italian tavern Chiappone, the meeting place of Dresden's literary circle. Drawn to such gatherings by his need for human contact, he usually found himself repelled by its unpleasant-ness, like the porcupines in his famous fable whose quills drive them apart when they get close to one another (*PP* II, pp. 651–2). As Baron Ferdinand Biedenfeld noted, Schopenhauer was always candidly honest, outspoken and resolute in discussion. But at the Chiappone a quarrel would usually begin and Schopenhauer could become aggressive, 'like a barking dog', angry and caustic (*G*, pp. 39–40).[10] Such outbursts earned him the nickname *Jupiter tonans* (thundering Jupiter) from Schulze. The painter Ludwig Sigismund Ruhl made a number of portraits of Schopenhauer in this period, the best – and best known – of which depicts the philosopher in a highly Romanticized image akin to those of Lord Byron. Closest to the philosopher was the wealthy landowner and art connoisseur Johann Gottlob Quandt, who had sought him out after meeting Johanna and Adele at Karlsbad in 1815. Though he was candid about his low opinion of Quandt's intellectual abilities, Schopenhauer developed an enduring affection for him, even suggesting to Adele many years later that she consider marrying the landowner.

Ludwig Sigismund Ruhl, *Schopenhauer* (aged 27), 1815, oil on canvas.

Schopenhauer's social relationships took second place to his philosophical calling. He carefully preserved and organized the worksheets written in Dresden; and in 1849 he added a note indicating that they

> show the fermentative process of my thinking, from which at that time my whole philosophy emerged, rising gradually like a beautiful landscape from the morning mist. Here it is worth

noting that even in 1814 (in my 27th year) all the dogmas of my system, even the important ones, were established. (*MR* I, p. 122)

The claim that all the dogmas of his philosophy were established by 1814 seems to jar with the poetic image of fermentative process and gradual emergence from the mist. It is also an exaggeration. Nonetheless, it is undoubtedly true that 1814 was the *annus mirabilis* in which the light cast by Plato, Kant and Indian religion revealed to Schopenhauer the main structure of his mature philosophical system.

Schopenhauer had started reading texts on ancient Indian religious thought in the winter of 1813–14 after meeting Friedrich Majer, the Orientalist scholar, in his mother's salon; he had probably been introduced to him by Goethe. Inspired by his friendship with Herder and other members of the Romantic movement to explore the origins of religion, Majer was one of the earliest German scholars to draw attention to the Upanishads, the Hindu scriptures that constitute the core of the Vedanta school of philosophy. Schopenhauer borrowed a two-volume edition of the Upanishads, entitled *Oupnek'hat,* from the Herzoglichen library in Weimar in March 1814, having already in December 1813 consulted issues of the journal *Asiatic Magazine* for 1802, which contained Majer's translation into German of an English version of the Bhagavadgita. He purchased his own copy of *Oupnek'hat* not long after his arrival in Dresden and over the years to come he fell under the spell of this curious text, a Latin version of a Persian translation of the original Sanskrit.[11] Towards the end of his life, he wrote that every page of this 'incomparable book' contained 'profound, original, and sublime thoughts . . . it has been the consolation of my life and will be that of my death' (*PP* II, pp. 396–7).

In one of the earliest notes to show the impact of his reading of Indian religion, written in Weimar prior to his move to Dresden, Schopenhauer combines both religious and philosophical terminology. Human life, he thinks, is 'doomed not merely to *sin* and *death*, but also to *illusion* (*Wahn*), and this *illusion* is as real as life, as real as the world of the senses itself, indeed it is identical with these (Māyā of the Indians)' (*MR* I, pp. 113–14). What is significant here is the characterization of the realm of empirical consciousness, 'the world of the senses', as *Wahn*, which can be translated in this context as illusion or delusion. Hitherto, following Kant, Schopenhauer had identified empirical consciousness as phenomenon, the world of appearance, in contrast to noumenon, reality-as-it-is-in-itself. This usage necessarily implies that sensory things are lacking in reality, not fully real. By identifying the world of the senses as illusion, Schopenhauer took a step towards the idealism of the Irish philosopher Bishop George Berkeley, while at the same time criticizing Kant for failing to admit the full implication of his own doctrine of the phenomenal world.[12] He encapsulated his brand of idealism in the claim that 'life is a long dream' (*WWR* I, p. 18): just as the brain conjures up dreamworlds during sleep, so too does it conjure up the everyday world of wakefulness (*WWR* II, p. 4). By identifying the world of the senses with appearance or phenomenon, then *Wahn*, illusion or delusion, and finally dream, Schopenhauer's idealism matches, as he frequently tells us (see *WWR* I, pp. 8, 17), the Hindu notion of the Veil of Māyā, which according to some interpretations is understood as the deceptive screen that enshrouds mortals throughout their lives and blinds them to the reality of their situation.

The Veil of Māyā can be lifted, pierced, seen through, by the enlightened. In Schopenhauer's terminology of 1814, it is the perspective of the better consciousness that allows acknowledgement of the illusoriness of everyday life. The enlightened achieve this insight, and the associated peace of mind, through disengagement from the business of living, retreat from willing life. Hence he endorsed Plato's view in the *Phaedo* that the entire life of the wise man is a long dying, a breaking away from the world. In line with the teachings of Hindu scripture, Schopenhauer identified our desires and cravings as the force that binds us in illusion (*MR* I, p. 114). His most general expression for that which ordinarily enslaves us in perpetual suffering is 'the will to life' (*MR* I, p. 98), a term that carries echoes of the work of many other thinkers of the time, including Fichte and Schelling, though at this stage in Schopenhauer's thinking it does not carry an excessively technical connotation. A crucial insight is that 'willing (the fundamental error) can never be satisfied': for, as Schopenhauer makes clear in one of the early notes he made in Dresden, obtaining the object of our desire will not bring satisfaction and put an end to our willing because new objects of desire will always arise. Release from willing 'occurs through better knowledge', a position Schopenhauer supports with a quotation from the *Oupnek'hat* (*MR* I, p. 130). The knowledge that stills desire is either an insight into the nature of things, such as the realization of the futility of the cycle of endless desires, or the calm contemplation of, for example, 'the beauties of nature, of landscape painting, the emotional side of still life' (*MR* I, p. 116). In such states, we are not subjects of willing; we are rather subjects of knowledge, pure timeless subjects aware of the eternal Platonic Ideas themselves.

> As the *subject of willing* I am an exceedingly wretched being
> and all our suffering consists in willing . . . On the other hand,
> as soon as I am wholly and entirely the *subject of knowing*, in
> other words am absorbed in knowledge, I am blissfully happy,
> wholly contented, and nothing can assail me. (*MR* I, p. 137)

Many pages of Schopenhauer's notes from this period are devoted to consideration of the nature of contemplation and aesthetic pleasure, thereby reflecting his own enjoyment of the rich collection of art in the Dresden art galleries as well as the beauty of the surrounding countryside.

Schopenhauer might well have believed that the philosophy he was creating had almost reached fruition. It appeared that he had successfully married his Kantianism with the duality of the better consciousness and the empirical consciousness he had derived from Plato in a way that conformed with the ancient teachings of Hinduism. What seemed to clinch the marriage between Plato and Kant, as he announced with a triumphant note, was the discovery which 'had not occurred to . . . anyone else, that Kant's thing-in-itself is nothing but the Platonic Idea' (*MR* I p. 143). But this was a serious confusion which led Schopenhauer into a cul-de-sac. As long as he persisted in this confusion, he was unable to see the deep significance of his great insight of 1814 that '*The world as thing-in-itself* is a great will which knows not what it wills . . .' (*MR* I, pp. 184–5). For if the Platonic Idea is identical with the Kantian thing-in-itself, and the thing-in-itself is (in some sense) will, then 'The will is the Idea' (*MR* I, p. 206). It is at just this point in his manuscripts of 1814, where he identifies will and Idea, that Schopenhauer later inserted the remark: 'this is incorrect'. He then neatly summarized the essential structure of his final system: 'the adequate objectivity of the will is the Idea, but the phenomenon is the Idea that has entered into the *principium individuationis*. The will itself is Kant's thing-in-itself' (*MR* I, p. 206; cf. p. 247).

Schopenhauer's realization that Kant's thing-in-itself is the will 'which knows not what it wills' was seminal in the development of his philosophy. By regarding the world as both will and representation, he preserved his allegiance to the Kantian dichotomy of thing-in-itself and phenomena. Plato's two worlds of Ideas and particulars were subsumed, together with the earlier conception of the better consciousness, into a new interpretation of the phenomenal world. The Ideas do not, as they do for Plato, comprise ultimate reality, reality as it is in itself; rather, they constitute the unchanging structure of the phenomenal world, the eternal forms of the world as representation, which are revealed to the pure knowing subject in the contemplation of art and nature. Particulars, the multiplicity of imperfect imitations of the Ideas, comprise objects in space and time interacting causally with one another, the objects of mundane consciousness dominated by the principle of sufficient reason. Since the scope of the principle of sufficient reason is confined to the world as representation, there can be no question, as Schopenhauer had demonstrated in his Dissertation, of regarding the thing-in-itself as the cause or ground of phenomena. Instead, as representations, phenomena are nothing but *appearances* of the thing-in-itself. Just as the colours and shapes of everyday objects are distorted in the eyes of someone wearing distorting spectacles, so thing-in-itself appears, in the light of the principle of sufficient reason, as a spatio-temporal world in the consciousness of a knowing individual (*MR* III, p. 160). The guise of the phenomenal world is what Hindu thinkers call the Veil of Māyā. Schopenhauer claimed to be the first philosopher to have provided an explanation of the nature of the disguise, though not the first person to have seen through it.

The World as Will and Representation resonates throughout with Schopenhauer's confidence and pride in his signal achievement in discovering 'the solution of the riddle of the world', the revelation that the thing-in-itself is will, will to life. This was the point on which Schopenhauer believed his philosophy definitively surpassed Kant's. He presents his great discovery in Book Two through consideration of the seemingly obvious point that a knowing individual is not, like some disembodied angel, merely an observer of the world; he is also a bodily creature who moves and acts in relation to other things. Thus, when sitting in the bath, I do not simply *see* my toes moving in the way that I see the movement of the trees outside the window: I *move* my toes. Moreover, the movements of my toes are not mysterious to me for the simple reason that they are *my movements*: my body moves at my will – I wiggle my toes. There is no need to investigate or infer anything, as we do with respect to the movement of the trees: I know immediately what I am doing in virtue of doing it. I wiggle my toes and I see them wiggling down at the end of the bath: and, Schopenhauer argues, what I do, wiggling the toes, is the same as what I see, the toes wiggling. There are not two causally related events taking place but 'one and the same thing, though given in two entirely different ways, first quite directly, and then in perception for the understanding' (*WWR* I, p. 100). To perceive the movements of your body in action is to observe an object in space and time known in accordance with the condition for knowledge of objects in general, that is, conformity to the principle of sufficient reason. But, Schopenhauer maintains, what is thus perceived is merely the outer aspect of what is immediately known to you from the inside as an act of will. Hence, he concludes, 'The action of the body is nothing but the act of will objectified, i.e., translated into perception' (*WWR* I, p. 100).

On the basis of this striking and original analysis of what it is to be an active embodied agent, Schopenhauer proceeds to draw a metaphysical conclusion that constitutes the heart of his philosophy. He takes 'the double knowledge we have of the nature and action of our own body' to be the key to 'the inner being of every phenomenon in nature' (*WWR* I, p. 105). For if what you know immediately in willing is not perceived in accordance with the principle of sufficient reason, it is not representation, not phenomenon; and if it is not phenomenon, it can only be the thing-in-itself (see *WWR* I, p. 110). That is to say, the thing-in-itself is revealed to us in willing. Granting the validity of this reasoning,[13] Schopenhauer proceeds to communicate his vision of the world as a restless inferno of endlessly striving phenomena. He relates animal behaviour and the behavior of inanimate things to human behaviour through a web of associations, thereby providing support for the extension of the concept of willing from the paradigm of deliberate human action to non-human activity. Thus animal behaviour exhibits willing even though, unlike human action, 'it is not guided by any knowledge' (*WWR* I, p. 114). The actions of animals are directed to goals of which they have no conscious awareness. 'The one-year-old bird has no notion of the eggs for which it builds a nest; the young spider has no idea of the prey for which it spins a web; the ant-lion has no notion of the ant for which it digs a cavity for the first time' (*wwr* I, p. 114). Human life, too, exhibits willing in the absence of forethought and deliberation, as when pain, and pleasure, prompt involuntary movements away from, and towards, their sources (*wwr* I, p. 101). And the impulses at work in human and animal behaviour are not fundamentally different from those found in lifeless phenomena. Drawing on the view he presented in his dissertation, that motives are causes seen from within, Schopenhauer comments on Spinoza's remark 'that if a stone projected through the air had consciousness, it would imagine it was flying of its own will. I add merely that the stone would be right' (*wwr* I, p. 126). That is, what we call our will is what is called brute force in inorganic matter. Understood in this light, Schopenhauer thinks it takes no great effort of imagination to see our own inner nature manifest in 'the powerful, irresistible impulse with which masses of water rush downwards, the persistence and determination with which the magnet always turns back to the North Pole, the keen desire with which iron flies to the magnet, the vehemence with which the poles of the electric current strive for reunion' (*wwr* I, p. 118).

It might be thought, as some have suggested,[14] that Schopenhauer's position would be less susceptible to misunderstanding if he used terms such as 'force' or 'energy' rather than 'will' to characterize the inner nature of all things. Yet this would have compromised the idealist character of the philosophy, steering it towards materialism, of which he was an avowed opponent. As Schopenhauer pointed out, concepts such as force are mere abstractions from what we observe in nature that is beyond explanation – we explain the movements of material bodies in terms of gravity though gravity itself is inexplicable – whereas will is a concept of what is most familiar to us and is grasped immediately by all knowing beings. Hence, Schopenhauer maintains, it is enlightening rather than obscurantist to see things in terms of will. 'Just as the first morning dawn shares the name of sunlight with the rays of the full midday sun', so what in human life is guided by 'the light of knowledge' is 'everywhere one and the same' with what in inorganic matter, 'the feeblest of its phenomena, only strives in a dull, one-sided and unalterable manner', and thus can bear the name of will (*WWR* I, p. 118).

With the 'key to the inner being of every phenomenon' securely in his grasp, from 1816 onwards the disparate elements of Schopenhauer's philosophy fell into place as he worked on the manuscript of *The World as Will and Representation.* By thinking of the world of representation as nothing other than the visibility of the 'blind, irresistible urge' (*WWR* I, p. 275) of the will-in-itself, the will to life, Schopenhauer was able to account for the bleak character of life and the world as he had come to know it. Conflict, suffering and death are not merely endemic but inevitable features of existence in the grip of the will. Just as at the lowest grades of material existence there is a never-ending struggle between natural forces such as gravitation and magnetism, so throughout the animal kingdom species compete against species for the necessities to maintain existence. Human beings who pride themselves on their reason and moral sense are no less driven by the will to life, their knowledge and forethought merely enabling them all the better to satisfy the savage egoism at the core of every character. Mired in illusion, nothing merely human can be of lasting value or meaningful. Within this nightmare vision, he found oases of tranquillity in aesthetic and moral experiences, deriving from knowledge that is no longer in the service of the will. And it is knowledge, too, knowledge which penetrates the Veil of Māyā, that leads to the quieting of the will and even to the denial of willing itself, denial of the will to life. Schopenhauer admits a path to salvation, though it is a path which leads nowhere and ends in nothing.

While Schopenhauer proclaimed the originality of his philosophy, early academic readers of his works pointed to its similarity with other post-Kantian philosophies. Yet in spite of the abuse Schopenhauer hurled at Fichte, Hegel and Schelling, the family resemblances between their work is not surprising in view of the common origin of their philosophies in Kant's critical philosophy. Thus, for example, they all espoused versions of idealism that take reality to be in some sense absolute, unitary and non-empirical. Schopenhauer did acknowledge 'the undeniable merit of Schelling in his *Naturphilosophie* (philosophy of nature)' (*PP* I, p. 24). Like Schopenhauer, Schelling made use of Plato's theory of Ideas to account for the ontology of the natural world and for the nature of art. Again, like Schopenhauer, Schelling understood the Absolute – spirit rather than will – to manifest itself as nature in which man evolves with self-consciousness. Where Schopenhauer does radically depart from his fellow idealists is in his assertion of the irrational character of reality. The world does not exhibit the unfolding of thought or reason, only the blind impulse to exist. The evolution of man's self-conscious is not the goal of Nature's perfection but another means for perpetuating existence. The will to life, which has no goal other than life, is the ultimate source of all the misery and suffering in life. In this way, Schopenhauer articulates a metaphysically grounded pessimism that is at odds with the metaphysically grounded optimism of the Absolute Idealists.[15] In his dethroning of reason, Schopenhauer was part of the Romantic reaction against the Enlightenment of the eighteenth century, and it was a theme later thinkers of the nineteenth century, such as Nietzsche, continued to develop.

Early in 1818, when the composition of *The World as Will and Representation* was nearing its end, Baron Biedenfeld contacted the publisher Friedrich Arnold Brockhaus on Schopenhauer's behalf to see if he would be prepared to accept it. Brockhaus had become a prominent figure in German publishing since rescuing the bankrupt *Conversations-Lexikon* in 1808, an encyclopaedia started in 1796. Schopenhauer was presumably unaware that Brockhaus was preparing to publish Johanna's latest volume of travel memoirs, to be followed in 1819 by her first novel, *Gabriele*. Perhaps it was the family connection with such a famous author that explained Brockhaus's apparent eagerness to take on Schopenhauer's volume of philosophy, an area in which the firm had few titles at that time. He regretted his decision, suspecting he was only printing waste paper. Schopenhauer proved to be an extremely awkward client – arrogant, impatient and insulting – and his book proved an economic liability for the company for many years.

Schopenhauer hoped that his work would appear in print in time for the autumn book fair. When it became clear that it would not, he set out on his planned holiday to Italy, entrusting his friend Quandt to take delivery of the ten author's copies promised in the contract. *The World as Will and Representation* appeared in December 1818 (bearing the date 1819 on its title page), by which time its author was in Rome. There he received a copy at the beginning of 1819 and was thrilled to see it, the 'fruit of his entire life'. His joy is understandable, for only twelve years earlier he had been labouring as a merchant's clerk, ill-educated and despairing of achieving the scholarly life he dreamed of. But his joy was short-lived. Soon he was to find his hopes dashed by disappointments, personal, professional and financial, that were to mark the beginning of a period of more than 30 years of increasingly bitter frustration.

Die

Welt

als

· Wille und Vorstellung:

vier Bücher,

nebst einem Anhange,

der die

Kritik der Kantischen Philosophie

enthält,

von

Arthur Schopenhauer.

Ob nicht Natur zuletzt sich doch ergründe?
Göthe.

....

Leipzig:
F. A. Brockhaus.
1819.

The title page of the first edition of *The World as Will and Representation*, 1819.

5

The Art of Genius

Schopenhauer's visit to Italy, like those of many other German intellectuals of the period, was partly inspired by his reading of Goethe's *Italian Journey* (1817), in which Goethe recounted his own experiences of the country and its culture 30 years earlier. However, for Schopenhauer Italy, at least on his first visit from 1818–19, was not the scene of aesthetic and intellectual revelation it had been for Goethe. The notebook he kept, the so-called 'travel diary' (*MR* III, pp. 3–66), is filled with further reflections on his familiar philosophical preoccupations and contains relatively few impressions of his new surroundings; it was not until his second visit from 1822–3 that he fully appreciated the charm of the Italian way of living.

Schopenhauer and his sister were passionate admirers of Lord Byron's poetry. For Schopenhauer, the admiration also extended to Byron's attitude to life in general and, more specifically, to women. Schopenhauer's works contain numerous references to Byron, including quotations from *Don Juan*, the great comic poem left incomplete by Byron's untimely death in 1824, whose opening cantos Byron was composing in Venice at the time of Schopenhauer's arrival there in October 1818. Schopenhauer failed to introduce himself to Byron, even though he possessed a letter of introduction from Goethe. His explanation, withheld from Adele, was his jealous fear of Byron, a fear prompted by the excitement the poet had aroused in Schopenhauer's latest *inamorata* – 'my Dulcinea' – on catching sight of him galloping past them on the Lido one morning

(*G*, p. 220). Doubtless Schopenhauer had not wished to reveal his 'regret' and 'stupidity' to Adele, though he was not as reluctant to conceal his amorous entanglements, even hinting on one occasion of the possibility of marriage. With proper sisterly devotion, Adele expressed the hope that Schopenhauer's infatuations with common women would not extinguish in him the capacity to genuinely value a woman, a concern that was not misplaced.

Schopenhauer's first child was born in the spring of 1819 to a lady's maid in Dresden. Adele noted in her diary that Schopenhauer was 'behaving well', but by late summer the child was dead. Confiding his affair to his sister helped rekindle the warmth in their relationship, which had cooled after the disastrous quarrel with Johanna. Adele lamented the child's death, for had she lived, Adele told Schopenhauer, he would have had someone to love and would not have been so alone.[1]

A letter written by Adele in February 1819 reached Schopenhauer in March, by which time he was in Naples, having spent the previous three months in Rome. She reported that Goethe was reading *The World as Will and Representation* with enthusiasm. Within hours of receiving his copy directly from her own hands in December 1818, Goethe had sent her a slip of paper communicating his thanks to the author and indicating some of the passages that had already given him special pleasure. These passages included Schopenhauer's view of the artist as anticipating the ideal character of beauty rather than imitating nature's imperfect manifestations of it (*WWR* I, pp. 221–2), and Schopenhauer's discussion of character in Book 4. Schopenhauer's pride in his achievement, bolstered by Goethe's flattering reception of his book, overflowed in a conceited verse composed on his return to Rome in April in which he announced that he knew 'that success [was] finally mine' and that 'posterity [would] erect a memorial to me' (*MR* III, p. 11). With such an elevated conception of himself, allied to his habitual outspoken truculence, Schopenhauer inevitably clashed with people who did not acknowledge his superior talent. This was particularly so in the German community in Rome, where he was known not as a distinguished philosopher but as the son who had quarrelled with his mother, the famous author. Members of this community, who included painters of the Nazarene movement dedicated to the revival of spirituality in Christian art, regularly congregated at the Caffè Greco, which Schopenhauer frequented, as if looking for trouble. On one occasion he provocatively praised Greek polytheism as a rich inspiration for artists and, when he was reminded that Christ had twelve apostles, shocked his listeners by his rude dismissal of the 'twelve philistines from Jerusalem'. On another evening, after he repeated his deeply held opinion that the Germans were the dullest of people, there was talk of having him thrown out (G, pp. 44, 46).

Apart from renewing his friendship from Göttingen days with the scholastic prodigy Karl Witte, Schopenhauer preferred the company of English tourists, especially as travelling companions. He returned once more to Naples and visited the classical ruins of Pompeii, Herculaneum and Paestum. In the Temple of Poisedon he was awestruck by the thought that he was walking where Plato's feet might once have trod. Thereafter he began his homeward journey, travelling via Venice and Milan where, early in June, he received a letter from a distraught Adele announcing that the Danzig bank in which she and Johanna had invested their capital had failed. Schopenhauer had deposited 6,000 thalers with Muhl, though, having prudently diversified his investments, this amounted to only around one-third of his assets. Schopenhauer immediately wrote to his mother and sister offering to share what remained of his fortune. The generosity of his offer was undermined by the inclusion of a spiteful note to his mother alleging that Johanna had in her treatment of her son and her daughter failed to respect 'the memory of that man of honour, my father' (GB, p. 42). So highly did Johanna value her freedom from male domination that she had already refused financial support from her friend Gerstenbergk and would no doubt have refused Schopenhauer's offer too. His insult stiffened her resolve but also provoked an angry scene with Adele in which Johanna said terrible things about her son – a few years later, she compared his offer of support to tossing alms to a beggar – as well as her late husband who, she felt, had compromised her independence by dividing his fortune between herself and the children rather than bequeathing it all to her. And yet, as Schopenhauer knew only too well, Johanna had, thanks to her grand style of life at Weimar, already worked her way through most of her own portion of the inheritance and had even started making use of her daughter's.

Adele was distressed to the point of contemplating suicide. She envisaged a future of impoverishment, perhaps at worst having to become a governess in Russia. With money borrowed from their friend Quandt, mother and daughter travelled to Danzig in the hope that their presence would enable them to take advantage of any opportunity that arose. Muhl proposed to his creditors that he could avoid bankruptcy if they would accept 30 per cent of their investment by way of settlement. Adele pleaded with Schopenhauer to accept. He refused. His suspicions were aroused, and he urged waiting for the banker to regain solvency. But Johanna and Adele could not afford the gamble: everything they possessed was at stake. They settled in May 1820, accepting a side payment of a small life annuity and some paintings.

Schopenhauer's native mistrust of other people's motivation, an attitude that bolstered his view of human nature as essentially egoistic, became paranoia in matters relating to his personal finances. The maintenance of his father's legacy, as well as being a sacred duty to his father's memory, was also a practical necessity if Schopenhauer was to continue his life as a scholar. In May 1821, exactly a year after the settlement deal, Schopenhauer wrote to Muhl demanding full payment of what was owed him together with interest. Muhl threw any number of sops in Schopenhauer's path in order to avoid handing over the money, including his life insurance policy and a flock of sheep, thereby confirming Schopenhauer's estimation of his character. But Schopenhauer was obdurate and pressed his claim relentlessly. Eventually, after Schopenhauer had threatened to sue, Muhl conceded, and Schopenhauer received 9,400 thalers in three separate payments. 'Observe that one can be a philosopher . . . without being a fool', Schopenhauer told Muhl (*GB*, p. 69). However, Schopenhauer's hard-headed commercial tactics did not prevent him from losing half the money he had recouped from Muhl a few years later through unwise investment in Mexican bonds.

Although Schopenhauer had presented his great work – the solution to the problem of existence – to the world, the world's response was not enthusiastic. He therefore decided that a position at a well-established university would enable him to present his philosophy directly to fresh young minds and to take a stand against the erroneous views of his contemporaries. Heidelberg, Göttingen and Berlin were the universities he considered. Contacting either a friend or a former teacher at each place to sound out his prospects of being accepted, Schopenhauer emphasized that as a scholar his interest was with 'the things that concern humanity equally at all times and in all countries' and not with contemporary politics or the 'machine of state' (*GB*, p. 45). In this way he gave assurance that he was no demagogue liable to fall foul of the Carlsbad Decrees established in 1819 by the states of the German Confederation to root out revolutionaries from state institutions. After careful assessment of the respective merits of the universities and their environments, he decided to apply to Berlin, since it was more receptive to philosophy than Göttingen, had a larger student body and was situated in a more cultured city. Moreover, Hegel was in Berlin and, having recently been appointed to Fichte's chair, was now the pre-eminent figure in German philosophy.

G.F.W. Hegel
(aged 58), 1828,
a lithograph after
a watercolour by
Julius Ludwig
Sebbers.

When Schopenhauer formally petitioned the University of Berlin at the end of 1819 to be considered for a teaching post in philosophy, he cheekily requested that his proposed course of lectures on 'general philosophy' be advertised as soon as possible so that he could deliver them in the forthcoming summer semester, at the same hour in which 'Herr Professor Hegel' would give his main course (*GB*, p. 55). The habilitation, or qualifying test, consisting of a lecture followed by discussion with members of the faculty, took place in March 1820. Hegel was present, though there is no way of knowing whether he had read the three books (the dissertation, the theory of colour and *The World of Will and Representation*) that Schopenhauer had submitted as specimens of his work, or indeed whether Schopen-

hauer had at this time read any of Hegel's work.[2] Hegel asked
Schopenhauer a question about what he said in the lecture on
motives in animals and there ensued, judging by Schopenhauer's
later report,[3] the sort of brief but testy exchange not uncommon in
academic life in which both parties succeeded in misunderstanding
one another. Schopenhauer believed himself to have exposed Hegel's
ignorance on this, the only occasion on which the two men met face-
to-face. Yet Hegel was the indisputable victor in their next contest.

Having passed his habilitation (with Hegel's vote in favour), the
new *Privatdozent* prepared himself to take on the Herr Professor
with a series of lectures on the philosophy of the world as will
and representation under the heading of 'general philosophy, i.e.,
the theory of the essence of the world and the human spirit'.[4]
Schopenhauer's confidence in the power of his philosophy and in
his own as yet untried ability as a lecturer received a shattering
blow. Hegel, at the height of his fame and popularity, attracted
an audience of about 200, whereas Schopenhauer, unknown and
inexperienced, found himself speaking to five students. And as the
weeks passed, that figure did not grow: it gradually diminished to
the point where neither students nor lecturer appeared in the hall.
He allowed his lecture course to be advertised almost every year
for the next decade, but he never lectured again. Even though there
is no necessary connection between being a great philosopher or
great writer and being a successful lecturer – Hegel himself had a
reputation as a poor lecturer – Schopenhauer's character prevented
him from accepting his failure gracefully. He attributed the collapse
of his career as a teacher, totally unjustly, to machinations by
Hegel and his university associates. Thereafter, Hegel assumed
for Schopenhauer the status of a hate-figure, someone on whose
name he could pour out the frustration and bitterness he felt at the
neglect of his philosophy in German universities. Schopenhauer's
subsequent publications, even the new editions of his previous
publications, are stained by streams of invective – admittedly,

highly inventive invective – against Hegel's person, his philosophy, his writing style and his influence on German culture.

Schopenhauer's venom was directed as much towards what Hegel represented in the intellectual life of Germany at the time as it was towards the defects in his philosophical works. For a philosopher, according to Schopenhauer, the pursuit of truth is paramount, whereas a professor, in order to retain his position as a paid employee of the state, is obliged to say and do nothing which would upset the authorities, such as contradicting established religious doctrines. 'It has, therefore', Schopenhauer commented sarcastically in a late essay, 'On Philosophy in the Universities', 'been one of the rarest events for a genuine philosopher to be at the same time a lecturer on philosophy' (*PP* I, p. 141). To Schopenhauer, the fact that Hegel's philosophy chimed so fittingly with the spirit of the times, a spirit of optimistic idealism, was simply evidence of Hegel's preference for preferment over truth. Hegel's copious use of Christian terminology to present his view of reality as a dynamic process in which God or the Absolute rationally unfolds itself in historical stages progressing inevitably towards the good was anathema to Schopenhauer, conflicting radically with his own pessimistic vision of an essentially immoral, non-rational universe. And yet, if Hegel's rise to the top of the academic tree is partly explained by the convergence of his philosophical views with the conventional wisdom of the day, then the neglect of Schopenhauer's philosophy in the same period is understandable. However, *The World as Will and Representation* was not completely ignored by the academic world: it was reviewed seriously but critically. None of the reviewers was a Hegelian; indeed, one, Johann Herbart, the holder of Kant's chair at Königsberg, criticized the work for deviating from Kantianism. Schopenhauer did cherish one review, the only one that came close to providing what he wanted, written in 1824 by the celebrated novelist and apostle of the Romantic movement Jean Paul, who praised *The World as Will and Representation* for its genius and profundity. Even so, he declined to recommend it on account of its desolate melancholy.[5]

Having failed to achieve the success and fame he had hoped to gain from the publication of his great work and from his lectures at the University of Berlin, Schopenhauer began a slow and painful process of readjustment. In his early thirties, he thought of himself as living in the second half of his life, a time in which, he believed, the naive and never-fulfilled desire for happiness is replaced by the fear of unhappiness, 'which is only too often fulfilled' (*MR* III, p. 64). Moreover, according to his own views on creativity and genius, in the latter part of life a man is capable only of working out or clarifying great truths rather than discovering them. He continued, therefore, the task of clarifying the 'great truths' he had presented in *The World as Will and Representation* with the prospect of producing a second edition. This kind of scholarly activity would not require a solitary existence 'in ice and high mountains',[6] a necessity for the inception of genius, because it could be sustained within a more sociable life that might even include marriage. So Schopenhauer judged in the early 1820s, about the time that he started a love affair with a young woman called Caroline Medon. In the year 1821 he also became entangled in an affair of another kind with a somewhat older woman called Caroline Marquet. Both affairs fuelled Schopenhauer's misogyny.

Caroline the younger was a nineteen-year-old, dark-haired and vivacious chorus girl at the Berlin Opera who, the year before she met Schopenhauer, had given birth to a child fathered by the Privy Secretary Louis Medon, whose name she used thereafter. In spite of his ungovernable jealousy at Caroline's relationships with other men, Schopenhauer felt great affection for her and their affair was the longest of his life. After ten years, when he decided to leave Berlin in 1831, he invited Caroline to accompany him. She refused to join him, largely, it seems, because he insisted that she leave behind her second son, who had been fathered by an unnamed

An undated, anonymous sketch of Caroline (Medon) Richter, Schopenhauer's mistress in the 1820s.

'foreign diplomat' while Schopenhauer was travelling in Italy in 1822–3. Schopenhauer's determination not to support another man's child cost him his last opportunity to avoid a lonely and loveless old age, the fate his sister had feared for him. But Schopenhauer's will was implacable: at his death, almost 30 years later, he left 5,000 thalers to Caroline with the stipulation that none of the money should go to the second son.

Where many others had failed, Caroline Marquet succeeded in obtaining financial support from Schopenhauer against his will. However, their relationship was legal rather than personal. Frau Marquet, a 47-year-old seamstress, lived in the house at Niederlagstrasse 4 where Schopenhauer rented two rooms. In the summer of 1821, in the very period during which he outwitted the banker Muhl, Frau Marquet brought an action for damages against Schopenhauer, alleging assault and slander. After almost six years of litigation, this resulted in the philosopher being sentenced to pay most of the court costs and a sum of 15 thaler every quarter as maintenance for the seamstress. Although Schopenhauer disputed the charges against him, what he admitted to in his statement to the court in September 1821 is itself boorish and petty, and leaves an ugly blot on his reputation.

Frau Marquet was in the habit of meeting her friends in the anteroom common to Schopenhauer's rooms and those of a fellow lodger. Irritated by the sight and sound of women gossiping in an area that was rightfully his, Schopenhauer complained to his landlady. Returning to his rooms on 12 August, he encountered the women and asked them to leave. A little later, finding them still there, he insisted they go, whereupon Frau Marquet protested and refused to comply even though her friends did. Then Schopenhauer put his arms around her waist and, overcoming her strenuous resistance, dragged her out, throwing her things out after her. When the by now furious and screaming woman attempted to re-enter the anteroom in order to claim one of her possessions that Schopenhauer had overlooked, he dragged her out once more but in such a way that she fell to the ground. This much Schopenhauer admitted, though he denied Frau Marquet's allegation that he had seized her by the throat, torn off her bonnet, beaten her and kicked her. 'Such rough brutality is quite unthinkable given my character, position, and education' (*GB*, p. 76), Schopenhauer grandly declared, thereby overlooking the fact that what he had already confessed to was surely unacceptable for a man of his character, position and education. Schopenhauer evidently assumed that as a *Privatdozent* his superior social status to that of the seamstress would count in his favour, but Frau Marquet was as tenacious in pursuit of her revenge as he was in defence of his finances. Having been fined 20 thalers for causing minor injuries, Schopenhauer then faced a civil suit in which Frau Marquet claimed that her injuries had resulted in an affliction to her arm which made it difficult for her to carry on her profession as a seamstress. In a tortuous series of court cases, during which Schopenhauer's assets were at one stage attached, each victory by the defendant was appealed by the plaintiff until the final judgement in favour of Frau Marquet was handed down in May 1827. Thereafter Schopenhauer paid maintenance every quarter for the rest of her life. When she died in 1842 Schopenhauer borrowed a Latin tag to embellish her death certificate: '*Obit anus, abit onus*' (The old woman dies, the burden departs).

In May 1822 Schopenhauer set off for a holiday in Italy, confident of victory in the forthcoming court hearing of the first of Frau Marquet's appeals (which in fact found against him). Berlin had become oppressive due to its high cost of living and its dust-laden atmosphere, in addition to the loss of his hopes there and the irritation of the Marquet affair. He arrived in Florence early in September and stayed for the next eight months. Here he relaxed and became more sociable, though it was mostly the company of English nobles he sought. He savoured the delights of the Italian countryside as well as the idiosyncrasies of the Italians. Shamelessness, he decided with lighthearted indulgence, was the principal feature of the national character (*MR*, III, p. 184). Letters to his friend from student days in Gotha, Friedrich Osann, whom he had entrusted to be his 'eyes and ears' in Berlin, described how much he enjoyed himself acting as a 'servant to the Muses' in a leisurely study of Florentine art. Little of what he saw, and of what he thought about what he saw, is recorded in his notebooks, though many of the works of art he encountered, as on his first visit to Italy, found their way into the elaboration of his aesthetic theory in volume II of the second edition of *The World as Will and Representation*. Schopenhauer had worked out his theory of art and aesthetic experience long before he went to Italy, though he had seen a lot of Italian art in the galleries of the cities of Europe and, in particular, in the Gemäldegalerie of Dresden while writing *The World as Will and Representation*.

To put it in the most general terms, Schopenhauer thought the essence of art consists in the revelation of the timeless character of the phenomenal world. The various art forms, with the exception of music, achieve this by representing particular phenomena so as to facilitate awareness of the Platonic Ideas which the phenomena exemplify. The emphasis on the presentation of Ideas distinguishes Schopenhauer's theory of art from standard Romantic theories which emphasize the expression of emotion and feeling. Though he does not deny that emotion enters into aesthetic experience, its defining character for Schopenhauer is the achievement of a form of perceptual knowing that is radically different from mundane perception of phenomena in space and time. It is a mark of his greatness as a philosopher that he does not attempt to squeeze music into line with his account of the other arts; and his insight into its distinctive nature, leading him to regard music as the most powerful art form, inspired praise from many creative artists, among whom Wagner was pre-eminent.

As in so many other areas of philosophy, Schopenhauer's theory of art and aesthetic experience, though influenced by Kant's theory, ultimately diverged from it. Unlike Kant in the *Critique of the Power of Judgment* (1790),[7] Schopenhauer has little to say about aesthetic judgement. Nonetheless, disinterestedness, one of the conditions Kant identified as essential to aesthetic judgement, is crucial to Schopenhauer's understanding of aesthetic experience. For Kant, a judgement is disinterested if it is grounded on a delight or satisfaction that is free from both practical and moral interest in a represented object.[8] This notion lies behind Schopenhauer's explanation of how experience of an object becomes aesthetic when it is purged of, or rises above, all traces of our familiar everyday ways of attending to, or taking an interest in, things: in other words, when our experience is free from willing (*WWR* I, pp. 178–9). Schopenhauer here takes seriously what people say when they talk of being lost in contemplation of a flower or a landscape, or totally absorbed in a book, painting or film. In such experiences the natural object or artwork fills our consciousness, displacing, for the time being, our habitual concerns about ourselves, our hopes and fears for our well-being. Our attention is so focused on the object that our ordinary will-driven thoughts, desires and goals are set aside. We have, Schopenhauer wants to say, lost our individuality, our subjectivity, and become a clear mirror of the object, an experience in which the perceiver and the perceived are indistinguishable. As Eliot puts it,

> . . . music heard so deeply
> That it is not heard at all, but you are the music
> While the music lasts.[9]

This quasi-mystical characterization of aesthetic experience is enriched within the terms of Schopenhauer's metaphysics. There is a simultaneous transformation in both aspects of the experience, the subject who perceives and the object that is perceived. When the perceiver ceases to attend to the relations of the perceived object to himself or to other things – when, as Schopenhauer marvellously puts it, he no longer considers 'the where, the when, the why and the whither in things, but simply and solely the what' (*WWR* I, p. 178) – his viewpoint on the world is no longer conditioned by the principle of sufficient reason, the principle of individuation, and he perceives the essence of the object independently of its relations in time and space. He sees the object, as it were, from the point of view of eternity: that is to say, he perceives the Platonic Idea of the species to which the particular object belongs, for the particular object *just is* the timeless Idea refracted through the individuating conditions of space and time. Lost in contemplation of this particular rose, the perceiver becomes aware of the essence of roseness. And the perceiver, too, is transformed. For, making use of Spinoza's maxim that 'the mind is eternal in so far it conceives things from the point of view of eternity',[10] Schopenhauer argues that the knowing subject rises above its particular location in the here and now to attain the condition of 'pure, will-less, painless, timeless *subject of knowledge*' (*WWR* I, p. 179).

Schopenhauer's theory attempts to do justice to the familiar thought that aesthetic experience generally, and especially in art, is not frivolous but important, for it enables us to penetrate the trivial superficiality of daily existence, to sense something deeper, truer in our lives – in Wordsworth's phrase, 'to see into the life of things'.[11] Van Gogh's paintings of sunflowers are not simply pictorial records of the beautiful flowers the artist had looked at: they show us something more, the sunlike radiance which warms and illuminates. Aesthetic experience is typically pleasurable, a haven of tranquillity from the busyness of daily affairs. The experience is pleasurable, Schopenhauer explains, because it is will-less. That is, since willing is the source of pain in our lives, the absence of willing in aesthetic experience is felt as pleasure. Hence Schopenhauer was highly critical of paintings in a strongly realistic style, depicting delicious-looking food or provocatively draped nudes, because the arousal of the appetites of hunger and lust would tend to destroy the disinterestedness of the aesthetic state (*WWR* I, p. 208). In true aesthetic experience 'we celebrate the Sabbath of the penal servitude of willing: the wheel of Ixion stands still' (*WWR* I, p. 196).

Of course, the Sabbath is but a respite from the daily round: aesthetic experience is temporary, often fleeting. For the ordinary person, it may be a rare experience, all the more cherishable because of its rarity. Yet, Schopenhauer maintains, the artist, the man of genius, can enjoy aesthetic experience more frequently and at much greater length, and it is this pre-eminent ability that enables him to create works of art in which he can present the Ideas he has grasped in a way that makes it easier for others to comprehend them when they attend to the artworks. The man of genius, whether he be an artist or a philosopher like Schopenhauer himself, is a seer, a visionary, with a powerful imagination that frees him from attachment to what is given in sense perception. But whereas other people use their imagination in the service of the will, conjuring dreams and castles in the air in which to fulfil their selfish fantasies, thereby evading reality, the genius ignores his self-interest and employs his imagination in achieving a completely objective comprehension of reality as manifested in the Platonic Ideas. Schopenhauer thinks specifically about *men* of genius, for he believes that women 'always remain subjective', concerned with how things relate to themselves, and so possess only talent, never genius (*WWR* II, p. 392).

Schopenhauer recognized a scale of art forms arranged in a hierarchy corresponding to the timeless hierarchy of the Ideas underlying the structure of the natural world: architecture, which exhibits inorganic Ideas, ranks as the lowest of the arts, while historical painting and drama are the highest arts due to their presentation of the Ideas of knowing individuals (*WWR* I, pp. 212–13). But music does not appear in this hierarchy. If it did, it would appear as one of the lowest art forms, for its employment of instrumental sounds restricts its capacity for the representation of particular phenomena to such things as thunderstorms, birdsong and traffic noise. To think of music in that way would, Schopenhauer realized, be to overlook its 'serious and profound significance' for our inner lives. With respect to its effect on our feelings, he acknowledged that music is 'very much more powerful and penetrating' than the other arts (*WWR* I, p. 257). It achieves this effect precisely *because* it bypasses the Ideas, which are manifestations of the Will, and *directly* exhibits the Will itself. By not copying particular things in the perceptible world, but relying entirely on the resources of musical sounds alone, music is able to give immediate expression to the striving, surging, pulsing, driving force of the Will, the inner nature of all things. For this reason, music acts directly on the listener's will, 'i.e., the feelings, passions, and emotions of the hearer, so that it quickly raises or even alters them' (*WWR* II, p. 448).

On the basis of this insight into the 'inexpressible depth' of music, Schopenhauer was critical of views of music which treated it as merely decorative or as an adjunct to poetry. In this respect he was in tune with the conception of classical music that emerged in the nineteenth century in the wake of Beethoven. The composer is a man of the most profound wisdom: a Beethoven symphony, for example, is 'a faithful and perfect likeness of the essence of the world' (*MR* III, p. 62). Music is a universal language of feeling, more immediately accessible than conceptual language. Hence music written to a descriptive programme is a violation of its nature, just as extravagant spectacle and dancing in opera detracts from music's true aim. However, Schopenhauer's view that music expresses, and indeed stirs, all the human passions and emotions raises a problem concerning the enjoyment of music. As manifestations of willing, emotions are painful; given its hotline to our emotional lives, music ought then to be the most distressing of the arts. Schopenhauer's solution is to say that what music expresses is not particular phenomena, not specific feelings of sorrow or affliction, nor indeed happiness and joy, but rather the 'extracted quintessence' of these feelings: that is, 'joy, pain, sorrow, horror, gaiety, merriment, peace of mind *themselves*, to a certain extent in the abstract, their essential nature, without any accessories, and so without the motives for them' (*WWR* I, p. 261). Music is in this respect no different from the other arts: our response to it is not as a particular individual rooted in the messiness of daily life but as a pure subject forgetful of our mundane identity.

Schopenhauer adopted a similar solution to the problem presented by phenomena in nature and in art that are threatening or disturbing: an avalanche or a forest fire that could destroy life, the vastness of the night sky or a great cathedral dome that overwhelms us. Appreciation of such phenomena was understood in terms of the Sublime, a concept then in vogue in European thought. While Edmund Burke and other writers had provided psychologically appropriate descriptions of the experience, Schopenhauer agreed with Kant in thinking that they had not understood the metaphysical structure of the Sublime.[12] In Schopenhauer's view (*wwr* I, pp. 201–7) the invigoration and exaltation of the Sublime derives from the continuing struggle to maintain will-less knowing in the face of the threat to the human will posed by the object. Thus the experience of the Sublime has a two-fold character – an awful beauty, a delightful terror – because it includes the subject's awareness that the phenomenon is threatening or disturbing to *human existence in general*. The subject overcomes his individuality, as in the case of music, so that the threat is felt not personally – which would annihilate the experience – but, as it were, universally, 'without reality and remote from its pain' (*wwr* I, p. 264).

What experiences of the Sublime intimate to us is the vulnerability and insignificance of life. And the highest degree of this feeling, Schopenhauer explains in the second edition of *The World as Will and Representation*, is provided by tragic art, for tragedy presents us with

> the terrible side of life . . . the wailing and lamentation of
> mankind, the dominion of chance and error, the fall of the
> righteous, the triumph of the wicked; and so that aspect

of the world is brought before our eyes which directly opposes our will. (*WWR* II, p. 433)

Paradoxically, and puzzlingly, we take pleasure in tragedy, even regarding it, as Schopenhauer did, as the greatest of the literary arts. As a young man in Weimar in 1811, he had been deeply moved by Goethe's production of Calderón's *The Constant Prince* (1629), in which the Prince, a religious martyr, endures lifelong imprisonment but attains to a state of indifference to the world until 'through death he is simultaneously granted freedom from death'.[13] Yet the significance of tragic art, Schopenhauer argued, derives not merely from its ethical content but from the intrinsic character of our response to it. In rising above the terrible antagonism the depicted events display to life and to willing, we find pleasure in what opposes the will: we celebrate the denial of the will, and in so doing we acknowledge that life and the world are 'not worth our attachment to them' and are thus led into resignation (*WWR* II, p. 434).

Early in May 1823 Schopenhauer brought his Italian holiday to an end and began his journey homewards. There was no pressing reason for his return; he did not even seem to have a definite idea about what he was going to do once he had reached Germany. The holiday had been a success. As he wrote to Osann a year later, 'It was an enjoyable time and I shall always think back to it with pleasure' (*GB*, p. 92). Even so, he never again set foot in Italy. He travelled via Trent and Innsbruck where, evidently in good humour, he made a note on the gaiety and hilarity in all laughter as a supplement to his incongruity theory of laughter, which was originally buried in *The World of Will and Representation* in his long discussion of concepts and judgements (I, pp. 59–61).[14] By June he was in Munich, intending to continue his journey after a few weeks. But a year later he was still there, having been confined over the winter by a series of distressing illnesses.

Schopenhauer's winter of discontent was the prelude to years of restlessness which came to an end when he settled in Frankfurt in 1833. There he resigned himself to a life of obscurity devoted to the establishment of his posthumous reputation.

6

The Mystery of Compassion

'Haemorrhoids with fistula, gout and a nervous malady succeeded one another; I spent the whole winter indoors and suffered very much' (*GB*, p. 92). That was how Schopenhauer described the afflictions that prolonged his stay in Munich from 1823 to 1824. Symptoms of his condition included shaking of the hands, which interfered with his ability to write; total deafness in his right ear, the culmination of the hearing difficulties he had experienced for most of his life, and depression. He may have been suffering the effects of a venereal infection contracted in Italy or even earlier in Berlin. A year after his arrival in Munich, he took himself off for a month to the spring baths at Bad Gastein and had a couple of months at the fashionable summer resort of Mannheim before returning for the winter to Dresden, where he had experienced happy days. But the six years since he had left Dresden for his first Italian holiday had changed him. In his autobiographical notes, he wrote in 1825 that 'all the world found an astonishing change in me'. He had become 'systematically unsociable'. He had 'acquired an "eye for loneliness"', and decided not to waste time on inferior bipeds but to devote the rest of 'this fleeting life' entirely to himself (*MR* IV, p. 492).

    In the course of the next few years Schopenhauer concocted numerous projects for the translation of a variety of philosophical and literary texts. Had these projects succeeded they would at least have put his name before the educated public, which had little or no awareness of his identity as the author of *The World as Will and Representation*. He first proposed translations from English into German, perhaps because he had recently been enthusiastically reading the novels of 'the incomparable Sir Walter Scott' (*PP* II, p. 456). He chose Lawrence Sterne's *The Life and Opinions of Tristram Shandy* (1759–69), his favourite English novel, and two essays on religion by 'the admirable and excellent David Hume' (*MR* III, p. 194). Schopenhauer took comfort in the fact that Hume had had to wait until he was 50 before his philosophical works achieved the acclaim they deserved. In a draft preface, he sarcastically suggested that Hume would have had more success had he sacrificed the 'clarity, comprehensibility and definiteness of his own style' in favour of spreading 'a mysterious obscurity through ponderous and endless sentences and affected and strange words and expressions' (*MR* III, pp. 198–9). Both Hume and Stern employed their literary talents in forthright opposition to moral and religious bigotry, which was something that appealed to Schopenhauer. However, the publishers he approached did not take up his offer.

Because his assets had been attached by the court that had heard Caroline Marquet's latest appeal, Schopenhauer was compelled by financial necessity to leave his haven in Dresden in the spring of 1825 and return to the bustle and vexation of Berlin. There he fell back into some of his old habits. The affair with Caroline Medon resumed in spite of the fact that she had given birth to another man's child while Schopenhauer had been away. He readvertised his lecture course at the University, and with invincible stubbornness once again chose the same times at which Hegel gave his lectures, and once again failed to win an audience. One happy benefit of this failure was that Schopenhauer had spare time to teach himself Spanish, so he was able to read some of his favourite authors – Calderón, Cervantes, Gracián – in their native language. In 1829 he began work on a translation of a book of aphorisms plus commentary, *The Art of Worldly Wisdom* (1647) by the seventeenth-century Jesuit Baltasar Gracián, whom Schopenhauer admired for his pessimism and sceptical view of personal relations. Although he twice failed to secure a publisher, Schopenhauer completed his translation while living in Frankfurt in 1832. It was finally published in 1862, two years after his death.

Of all Schopenhauer's translation projects, the most important was his proposal to translate Kant's works into English. On reading an anonymous article in the British *Foreign Review and Continental Miscellany* for 1829 which spoke of the need for an English translation of Kant's first *Critique* and other works, Schopenhauer wrote suggesting himself for the task and enclosed a sample translation of Kant's *Prologemena* (*GB*, pp. 117–23).[1] When the author Francis Haywood proposed that they should translate the *Critique* together, Schopenhauer wrote to the publishers of the *Foreign Review* and repeated his proposal, pointing out that 'a century may pass ere there shall again meet in the same head so much Kantian philosophy with so much English as happen to dwell together in mine' (*GB*, p. 124). Sadly for the history of British philosophy, the publishers did not take up the proposal. However, in the late 1820s two of Schopenhauer's translation projects resulted in publications, though they were both so obscure that they did nothing to increase his reputation and brought precious little financial compensation. One was a short story, 'Der Prophet von St Paul' by Lord Norman, which was published in a British journal in 1830 and earned Schopenhauer the princely sum of 22 thalers. The other was a Latin version of *On Vision and Colours*, which was published in 1830 in a Leipzig journal, *Scriptores Ophthalmologici Minors*, and received no more attention than the original.

In spite of his abject failure as a university lecturer, Schopenhauer was not inhibited from trying to obtain posts at other universities. His desire to escape from Berlin, a city in which he disliked living, was compounded in the late 1820s by financial pressure stemming from losses on his investments in Mexican bonds coupled with a renewed desire to marry. In 1828 he wrote in his autobiographical notes that his 'desire to possess a wife who will wholly belong to me' required him to move to a country town where he would have no opportunity to buy books – which he could not afford if he were to marry and remain in Berlin (*MR* IV, p. 493). The expression 'possess a wife who will wholly belong to me' suggests that it may not have been Caroline Medon that Schopenhauer was thinking of, for he well knew of her relationships with other men, but Flora Weiss, the seventeen-year-old daughter of a Berlin art dealer, with whom he had become enamoured. When he sought permission to pay court to Flora, her father protested that she was merely a child, but Schopenhauer replied that this was what pleased him (*G*, p. 59). Flora, however, was revolted by the prospect of living in a country town married to an ageing philosopher who wooed her with stingy presents. Schopenhauer's suit foundered, as did his applications for university employment.

Any satisfaction Schopenhauer felt at the publication of *On Vision and Colours* in Latin was dwarfed by his despair over his failure to obtain publication of the second edition of *The World as Will and Representation*. The year 1828 marked the tenth anniversary of the publication of his great work and he drafted versions of a new preface as well as a heartfelt tribute to his father, to whom the new edition was to be dedicated. Enquiring of his publisher, the firm of Brockhaus, the extent of the sale of the first edition, he was shocked to discover that there were still unsold copies of the first printing in the warehouse even though an unspecified number had been pulped, a fact that meant that a second edition was impossible at the time.[2] This terrible blow was the final nail in the coffin of the hopes that had brought him to Berlin in 1820: he had failed to establish a university career, secure any kind of regular employment or find fame for his philosophical views or an audience for his writings. What remained was his indomitable conception of himself as a seeker of truth whose immortal works would one day be recognized. It is not surprising that his note-book of the period – aptly titled 'Adversaria' – was increasingly filled with reflections on the futility of life and the nature of death. 'Every human life', he decided, was a tragedy in which we see 'nothing but a series of disappointed hopes, defeated plans and errors realized too late' (MR III, p. 577); he concluded that 'life is obviously not worth the effort' (MR III, p. 580).

Schopenhauer endured Berlin until the summer of 1831, when he fled the city to escape a serious outbreak of cholera which soon claimed the life of Hegel. Curiously, Schopenhauer interpreted a dream of a long-dead school friend as 'a warning' that he would die of cholera if he remained there (MR, IV, pp. 61–2); however, though he experienced the dream on New Year's Eve 1830 he did not leave Berlin until the following August. In any event, he was in such a hurry to go that he left behind his library of books and the manuscript of his translation of Gracián, which he entrusted to his friend Baron Heinrich von Lowtzow. Immediately on his arrival in Frankfurt, Schopenhauer experienced what he described as, not a dream, but 'a perfectly clear spirit-phenomenon' or apparition in which both his parents appeared, his father carrying a light. It struck Schopenhauer that his father was conducting his mother on the path to death and that the experience indicated that he would outlive his mother (MR IV, p. 62). Schopenhauer's state of mind was evidently disturbed and over the next few weeks, living alone in the unfamiliar surroundings of Frankfurt, his condition gradually deteriorated into the depression and illness that kept him indoors for most of the winter. At this time he resumed correspondence with his sister and mother, who were now living in straitened circumstances in Bonn, after a silence of almost ten years. In addition to discussing their mutual financial worries he spoke of his poor health.[3] Johanna was shocked to hear in March of his grey hair and long beard and that he had not seen anyone for two months.[4]

It was not until the summer of 1832 that Schopenhauer roused himself. Taking his doctor's advice, he decided to move to Mannheim, a city of which he had fond memories, where he had recuperated after the bad winter of 1823–4. Once again the warmth and airiness of the Baroque city exerted its charm, going some way to restoring his spirits. He met friends he had made on his previous visit and even joined an association of local dignitaries optimistically entitled 'The Harmony Society', which had its own library. But if anything, for this constitutionally unsociable thinker, Mannheim was too sociable. It was certainly too crowded with visitors: he appreciated the anonymity provided by the bigger city of Frankfurt. In 1833 he began to reconsider the suitability of Mannheim as his permanent residence. Like the merchant's clerk he had once been, he drew up a balance sheet in English on the cover of his account book, itemizing the comparative advantages of Mannheim and Frankfurt. On balance, he preferred Frankfurt. While Mannheim had a lower danger of thieves and better baths in summer, it could become intolerably hot, whereas Frankfurt had a healthy climate – allegedly, cholera-proof – an able dentist and less bad physicians. Generally speaking, Frankfurt was a gayer place: it had better plays, concerts and operas, as well as better table-fare and coffee-houses. What Schopenhauer did not specify in his balance sheet was that unlike Mannheim, which catered for tourists in search of relaxation, Frankfurt was an imperial free city and a busy commercial centre, frequented by bankers and merchants from all over Europe. In both respects it was reminiscent of Danzig and Hamburg.

Having taken his decision to return to Frankfurt in such a coolly calculating manner, Schopenhauer was then struck by one of his recurrent fits of irrational terror. He recorded it in his autobiographical notes: 'As I was about to leave Mannheim in July 1833, I was overcome by an indescribable feeling of fear without any external cause' (*MR* IV, p. 507). This episode was prompted perhaps by his sense of the enormity of the commitment he was making;

for when he arrived in Frankfurt on 6 July, he had reached his final destination on earth. Frankfurt was where he died in 1860, never having left the city during the intervening years for more than a few days at a time. Frankfurt was also the place where his way of life solidified into the rigid routines of the confirmed bachelor. Entries in his autobiographical notes for 1831 (*MR* IV, pp. 502–6) show that he had decided, after considering its merits and demerits, against marriage. Though his desire for companionship did at times impel him to act against his considered judgement, as when he invited Caroline Medon to leave Berlin with him, it gradually gave way to a haughty pride in his lack of dependence on what he regarded as the unwise and unintelligent half of mankind. He conceded that his temperament was such that it was unlikely his wife would be happy with him. Moreover, he, like all genuine philosophers of the modern era, required peace, quiet and seclusion in order to achieve the higher intellectual goals to which his life was devoted. He was eventually able to condense his deliberations on marriage into a memorably mischievous maxim: 'Matrimony = war and want! Single blessedness = peace and plenty!' (*MR* IV, p. 505).

Schopenhauer's anxieties about marriage would not have been unusual for men of his age, class and education in Europe of that period, though lurking beneath his notes are his metaphysical views on gender and sexuality, thinly covering his bitterness towards his mother. Both coalesced more vividly in Schopenhauer's late – and now notorious – essay 'On Women', first published in 1851 in *Parerga und Paralipomena* (II, pp. 614–26). Schopenhauer thought there was little to be said in favour of women, apart from their admittedly indispensable capacity for bearing and rearing children and for comforting and nursing men in illness and old age. They are well-suited for these roles because, among other things, they are more compassionate than men: although Schopenhauer regards this attribute as a simple consequence of women's weakness at reasoning and thinking. As he puts it, 'they are themselves childish, trifling and short-sighted, in a word, are all their lives grown-up children' (*PP*, II, pp. 614–15). Deficient in reason, women are dominated by feelings, and so are incapable of the kind of objectivity necessary for artistic genius and great intellectual labour. Schopenhauer does not merely give expression to such preposterous beliefs: he relishes the opportunity to express them in a scornful and humiliating fashion. And his language becomes more aggressive in tone when discussing matters of sexuality.

> Only the male intellect, clouded by the sexual impulse, could call the undersized, narrow-shouldered, broad-hipped and short-legged sex the fair sex; for in this impulse is to be found its whole beauty. (*PP*, II, p. 619)

Here women are presented as the object rather than the cause of men's delusion, which itself arises, on Schopenhauer's own theory, out of the will's craving for existence. As he explained in his essay 'The Metaphysics of Sexual Love' (*WWR* II, pp. 531–67), love between men and women is merely the disguise employed by nature in its determination to propagate the species: what really draws Romeo to Juliet is the unborn child.[5] Because women fundamentally exist for the purpose of bearing children, Schopenhauer maintains that everything a woman does pertains to capturing a man. As the weaker sex, women cannot rely on force and have to resort to lies and cunning. Dissimulation is as natural to women as tusks in elephants, and teeth and claws in lions, and is invariably accompanied by 'falseness, faithlessness, treachery, ingratitude, and so on' (*PP* II, p. 617). This confrontation between the sexes is aggravated, Schopenhauer argues, by the practice of monogamy. The laws associated with monogamous marriage halve men's rights and double their duties and, by implying that women are the equal of men, elevate some women to the absurd status of lady and reduce others either to useless old maids or to those who make themselves available to gratify men's sexual desires. He advocates polygamy as more appropriate to both sexes, since it satisfies man's need to have many women, whom he is then obliged to support, and restores woman to her natural and proper position 'as a subordinate being and the *lady*, that monster of European civilization and Christian-Germanic stupidity with her ridiculous claims to respect and veneration, disappears from the world' (*PP* II, pp. 624–5).

Given his views on women, it is fortunate that Schopenhauer never became a husband. His constant companions in Frankfurt from July 1833 were, as ever, his books, flutes and dogs. He had owned numerous poodles since his student days in Göttingen, most of them called Atma after the Hindu name for the universal spirit or world soul. Schopenhauer preferred poodles to people. They gave him the unquestioning loyalty and love that he never received from anyone else, and in return he gave them the care and affection he was loath to offer to his fellow bipeds. He was especially fond of one Atma, a white poodle he owned for almost ten years, referring to it in the second edition of *The Fourfold Root* as 'my very intelligent poodle' (p. 110). Its sudden death in 1849 caused him intense grief. Its immediate successor, a brown poodle, outlived him, though he had made provision for it in his will.

Schopenhauer's affection for his poodles was one manifestation of his more general concern for the welfare of animals. The suffering and torments animals endure at the hands of men sickened Schopenhauer and contributed to his loathing of mankind and of religions, Christianity especially, that condoned such cruelty. Unlike most Western philosophy in which animals are regarded as mere means for human ends, Schopenhauer's philosophy regarded the nature of animals as fundamentally the same as man's, since both are nothing but manifestations of the Will. 'The eternal essence . . . exists in every living thing, and shines forth with inscrutable significance from all eyes that see the sun' (*BM*/*TPF*, pp. 96/162). As willing creatures, just like humans, animals have

Wilhelm Busch, an 1860s sketch of Schopenhauer with his poodle.

feelings and emotions; and it is their capacity for suffering that entitles them to moral consideration and respect. '*Tat tvam asi*' (this thou art), the Hindu and Buddhist expression for the inner identity of all living things, is the principle that should guide our conduct with animals, he argued. Even so, he did not condemn the eating of meat, for he believed a meat diet was necessary for people in the colder northern hemisphere. But our duty towards animals requires that their deaths should be brought about as painlessly as possible (*PP* II, p. 375). Schopenhauer was vehement in his denunciation of what he saw as – and as his pioneering teacher, Johann Blumenbach, had argued at Göttingen – the barbaric atrocities perpetrated on animals by unnecessary and futile experiments in the name of scientific research (*PP* II, pp. 373–5). The English, he maintained, had shown Europe the right path by establishing a society for the prevention of cruelty to animals, and he was active in support of similar schemes in Germany.

Schopenhauer's poodles figure in the regular lifestyle he established during his Frankfurt years: they accompanied him in all weathers on a two-hour brisk walk which began about four o'clock every afternoon. Like Kant in Königsberg at the end of the eighteenth century, his daily routine was inflexible. Unlike Kant he was not an especially early riser, since he maintained that the need for sleep was directly proportional to the intensity of cerebral life (*MR* IV, p. 138). Schopenhauer left his bed between seven and eight o'clock and devoted the morning to his work. Noon was the signal for thirty minutes' relaxation with his flute before he prepared himself to take lunch at one o'clock at the *Englischer Hof*. Like his heroes, Kant and Goethe, he was a hearty eater, his theory being that a large appetite fuelled great mental exertion. Lunch over, he would return home for a short nap and some lighter reading before setting out on his 'constitutional'. Then there would be a visit to the reading-room to peruse *The Times* newspaper and other periodicals, whereupon he would take himself off to a play or concert. Between eight and nine he would have a cold supper with a half-bottle of light wine, and return home, where his reading, while smoking an elongated pipe for the hour before bed, would invariably include the *Oupnek'hat*. It was only towards the end of his life, during the years of fame from 1854–60, that other people would enter into these routines, either by visiting him before lunch or accompanying him on his walk. But even before his celebrity days, Schopenhauer and Atma (or 'young Schopenhauer', as the dog was known to local children) had become familiar to residents around the Schöne Aussicht, near the bridge over the Main, where he lived from 1843.

In 1833 Schopenhauer's offer to serve as proofreader for a French publication of Goethe's writings was rejected, but he was successful when in 1837 he persuaded the editors of a new edition of Kant's collected works to publish the first edition of *The Critique of Pure Reason* of 1781 rather than the substantially revised edition of 1787. Schopenhauer realized, after discovering the first edition in 1826, that Kant had mutilated 'the most significant book ever published in Europe' (*GB*, pp. 167) in his attempt to eliminate his commitment to idealism. The revision, with its new section, 'The Refutation of Idealism', was, as Schopenhauer had argued in the Appendix to *The World as Will and Representation*, inconsistent in its treatment of idealism. 'In truth', he informed the editors, 'the second edition is like a man of whom one has amputated a leg and replaced it with a wooden one' (*GB*, p. 166). It was a signal triumph for Schopenhauer that the editors accepted his case: the first edition of Kant's *Critique* was published in Rosenkranz and Schubert's edition of Kant's collected works (Leipzig, 1838–42), the twelfth volume of which contained an essay on the history of Kantian philosophy written by Rosenkranz, which characterized Book Four of *The World as Will and Representation* as a 'sublime, deeply affecting poem' containing 'magnificent, genuine mysticism'.[6] Here, at last, was genuine praise for *The World as Will and Representation* from Germany's philosophical establishment.

Schopenhauer made use of some of the extensive manuscript notes and observations he had accumulated since 1818 when in March 1836 he published the small book *On the Will in Nature*. Its ponderous subtitle, 'A Discussion of the Corroborations from the Empirical Sciences that the Author's Philosophy has received since its first Appearance', is indicative of Schopenhauer's motivation for publishing the book: that he might be able to draw favourable attention to *The World as Will and Representation* if he could show that recent advances in the sciences were in accord with the philosophy of nature he had advanced in Book Two. In a characteristically brilliant image, he suggests that he and the scientists were like

> miners in the bowels of the earth who drive two galleries toward each other from two widely separated points, and who, having long worked from both directions in subterranean darkness and relied only on compass and spirit-level, at last experience the longed-for joy of hearing each other's hammer blows. (*WN*, p. 22)

The metaphor here misleadingly suggests that the scientist and the philosopher work on the same level. But it was Schopenhauer's view that the philosopher goes deeper than the scientist. The physicist's explanations of phenomena will come to an end with the recognition of the ultimate forces of nature, gravity, electricity, etc. At this point the task of the metaphysician begins: to find explanations for what the physicist has to take for granted, thereby filling out and completing our understanding of the nature of existence. This is exactly what Schopenhauer believed he had achieved with his metaphysics of the will – it was not merely consistent with what science had discovered, but finally made sense of the picture of the world provided by science. Five hundred copies of *On the Will in Nature* were printed by the Frankfurt publisher Siegmund Schmerber; a year later 375 remained unsold. The book was even less successful than *The World as Will and Representation* and received only two unenthusiastic reviews.

Since commencing his higher education at Göttingen, Schopenhauer had always interested himself in the latest developments in the sciences, and in Frankfurt it was at the Senckenberg Library that he found the resources to maintain this interest. Of the eight chapters that comprise *On the Will in Nature*, the first four concern the natural sciences, while the remainder deal with linguistics, animal magnetism and magic, sinology and ethics. Schopenhauer's usual procedure is to find a quotation from a scholarly work on these topics that employs some notion of will and then to show how this concurs with aspects of his own philosophy of will as the inner nature of all phenomena. Thus, in the chapter on physical astronomy, he quotes from the *Treatise on Astronomy* of 1833 by the English astronomer John Herschel, who maintained that the force of gravity is the result of 'a consciousness and a will existing somewhere, though beyond our power to trace'. Herschel's mistake was his belief that will is inseparable from consciousness, a mistake that Schopenhauer had already pointed out in *The World as Will and Representation* (*WN*, pp. 85–8). Furthermore, he argued that even in cases of great scientific success in understanding causal transactions, there was, as the quotation from Herschel illustrated, always an unknown factor, an inner essence that had not been grasped. It was just this unknown factor that Schopenhauer's philosophy identified as will, manifesting itself obscurely in material phenomena and more clearly in the self-consciousness of knowing beings (*WN*, p. 94).

The longest chapter in *On the Will in Nature* is entitled 'Animal Magnetism and Magic' (pp. 102–28), a title which would be equivalent in contemporary terminology to 'hypnotism and the paranormal' or, more simply, 'the occult'. Schopenhauer's understanding of the Kantian doctrine that causal laws between objects in space and time are mere appearances rather than absolute reality enabled him to look sympathetically on all kinds of so-called paranormal experiences – clairvoyance, mind-reading, telekinesis, spirit-seeing. Schopenhauer also sincerely believed that he himself had had genuine experiences of pre-cognition and spirit-seeing, and he was in the vanguard of those scientists and philosophers in the nineteenth century who were prepared to subject such experiences to rational enquiry. As a new *Privatdozent* in Berlin, Schopenhauer had been allowed by the Professor of Medicine, Karl Christian Wolfart, to visit his somnambulist patients to see for himself the efficacy of magnetism in the treatment of illnesses, a technique that had been pioneered in the eighteenth century by the Austrian physician Franz Anton Mesmer. For Schopenhauer, what was crucial was the will of the magnetizer (*wn*, p. 103). Indeed, he believed he had 'magnetized' one of Wolfart's patients merely by looking at her (*g*, p. 262). He maintained that magnetism was akin to magic, which produces effects in the physical world in defiance of established causal laws. Both were intelligible in the light of his philosophy of will, for, underlying the hocus-pocus of the magician, just as under Mesmer's play with magnets, there lay the magician's will, which exploited 'a *nexus metaphysicus*' (*wn*, p. 112) to influence events. Schopenhauer did not discount the possibility of deceit and mis-representation, yet despite his parade of scholarly rigour in sifting evidence concerning the paranormal, his writing on this topic is embarrassing for the credulity he displays towards what appears to modern readers as patent fraudulence.

The year of the publication of *On the Will in Nature*, 1836, was also the year in which Charles Darwin returned to England after the voyage of the *Beagle*, during which he had amassed the biologi-cal data that enabled him to develop his theory of evolution. When Schopenhauer read a detailed account in *The Times* of *The Origin of Species* (1859) early in 1860, he dismissed Darwin's work as 'just stale empiricism', nothing more than a variation of Lamarck's theory of the inheritance of acquired characteristics (*gb*, p. 472). Schopenhauer was mistaken in thinking that Darwinism is simply a variation of

Lamarckism, yet he rightly saw that Darwin's empiricist theory of the evolution of species was incompatible with his own idealist metaphysics of the unchanging character of the species enshrined in the Platonic Ideas. Schopenhauer can sound very like Darwin when he talks of the struggle for existence, the adaptation of the organism to its environment and the maintenance of the species. The resemblance reflects his grasp of developments in biology that also influenced Darwin. But, for Schopenhauer, adaptation is explained teleologically by the organism striving to conform to the Idea of the species, which is given a priori by the will outside time. It is precisely this goal-directed form of explanation that is overthrown by Darwin's mechanical explanation of the evolution of new species in terms of natural selection, which allows some individuals to survive and reproduce more successfully than others when they possess variations that enable them to adapt to their environment.[7]

Schopenhauer's mother died on 16 April 1838. Johanna had not been in good health since surviving a stroke in 1823, and she and Adele had lived in genteel poverty since the collapse of the Muhl bank. In spite of the success of Johanna's writings, she received insufficient remuneration from them, and financial stringency forced the pair to leave Weimar in 1829 in search of more economical living conditions. They settled in Bonn, but by 1837 they were struggling and Johanna petitioned the Grand Duke of Saxony-Weimar, the successor to Carl August. He awarded her a modest pension that enabled them to live respectably in Jena, close, but not too close, to their old friends. There Joanna worked on her memoirs. Unfinished at her death, these ironically ended at the birth of the son with whom she had so violently quarrelled.[8] It had been 24 years since Schopenhauer had last seen his mother. But he did not attend her funeral; nor did he dispute her will, which left her estate, her land in Ohra and 2,000 thalers to Adele.

Just as her husband's death had liberated Johanna, so her mother's death freed Adele from her role as companion and nurse. She indulged her long-cherished desire to travel, in particular to Italy, and developed her literary talent, publishing stories and collaborating on a libretto. In the absence of their mother, the children drew closer together, though they did not meet again until 1842.

At the time of his mother's death, Schopenhauer was hard at work on his essay *On the Freedom of the Will*, which he intended to submit to the essay competition announced in April 1837 by the Royal Norwegian Society of Sciences on the question 'Can the Freedom of the Will be Proved from Self-Consciousness?' Under the condition of anonymity which precluded mention of his own publications, Schopenhauer had to address the issue of freedom in its own right, refraining from articulating his metaphysics of the will. He submitted the essay in June 1838, and in January 1839 the Society awarded him its gold medal as the winner of the essay competition. This was Schopenhauer's first taste of success and his pride in his achievement was immense. But if he thought this was the beginning of real fame, he was soon to be disabused. In July 1839 he submitted another essay, *On the Basis of Morality*, to a competition previously announced by the Royal Danish Society for Scientific Studies on the question '*Is the source and foundation of morality to be looked for* in an idea of morality which lies immediately in consciousness (or conscience) . . . ?' (*BM/TFP*, p. 38/114). The Society delivered its verdict in January 1840. It did not award the first prize to Schopenhauer's essay – or to any other. His had been the only essay submitted for the competition! Alleging the weakness of his arguments, the Society also gave as a reason for refusing him the prize Schopenhauer's indecent remarks about several eminent philosophers of the modern age. Greatly angered, Schopenhauer wasted no time in publishing both his competition essays under the title *The Two Fundamental Problems of Ethics* (1841), proudly indicating on the title page that the essay on freedom had been 'crowned with a prize' and that the essay on the basis of morality had 'not been crowned'. In the preface he ferociously lambasted the Danish Society, rebutting its criticisms of his work as well as justifying his abuse of the eminent philosophers Fichte and Hegel.[9] Twenty years later, not long before he died, when he came to write the preface to the second edition of the book, Schopenhauer was still angry and lashed out just as violently.

The two essays that comprise *The Two Fundamental Problems of Ethics* present Schopenhauer's ethical views in a more accessible manner than Book Four or the supplementary essays in volume II of *The World as Will and Representation*, for he was not concerned in the essays, as he had been in *The World as Will and Representation*, with working through the details of his metaphysics. Yet the essays are designed to lead the reader to a recognition of the need for meta-physics: Schopenhauer thought that the nature of freedom and morality have to be ultimately comprehended with reference to Kant's distinction between empirical and intelligible character. Though he regarded this distinction as 'one of the most beautiful and profound ideas brought forth by that [Kant's] great mind, or indeed by men at any time' (*FW/TFP*, pp. 96/107), Schopenhauer nevertheless rejected 'the absolutely *a priori* nature' of Kant's moral philosophy. Since for Schopenhauer reason is secondary to willing in human life, a morality grounded on purely rational principles would be ineffectual. Hence, Schopenhauer claimed, the notorious Categorical Imperative, the alleged supreme principle of morality, is nothing but the form of a law without substance, lacking motivational force for men 'in the storm and stress of life' (*BM/TFP*, pp. 75/145).

Like the sceptics of ancient Greece so derided by Plato, and those of modern Europe, such as Hobbes, Schopenhauer recognized that most people obey laws and do what is considered right out of some self-interested motive such as fear of punishment, human or divine. The state is not, as Hegel conceived it, a quasi-religious institution necessary for the achievement of man's higher spiritual illumination, but merely a rational device for maximizing the welfare of groups of people. Yet Schopenhauer was no moral sceptic. He acknowledged that sometimes people act out of compassion for the good of others and even out of malice. Compassionate acts, he thought, were rare but nonetheless real. Since it conflicts with the deep-rooted egoism natural to all living things, Schopenhauer calls compassion 'the great mystery of ethics' (*BM/TFP*, pp. 144/201): compassion does not depend on the individual's free choice but flows from the depths of his character.

Schopenhauer argued that freedom of will is illusory. He does not deny that we *act* freely when we act without internal or external constraint. In such a case we do what we want, what we will. But this does not establish that we are free to will what we will; that is, to will a different action in the very same circumstances (*FW/TFP*, pp. 18–19/43–4). For actions, like all events in the phenomenal world, have sufficient causes: given an individual character, together with a specific motive in certain circumstances, only one action is possible. Schopenhauer regards the feeling that we are free when we choose as an illusion arising out of our awareness of conflicting motives. When Schopenhauer deliberated about making Mannheim or Frankfurt his permanent residence, the will to move to Frankfurt arose out of his character, his inner nature as a willing being, accompanied by the consciousness of alternatives that created the illusion that some other willed action was possible.

The absence of free will also conflicts with our feelings of responsibility for our actions and with the deep sense of guilt felt for 'things ill done and done to others' harm'.[10] Schopenhauer does not regard these promptings of conscience as illusions. On the contrary, he takes them as direct evidence of ownership of our actions, 'the feeling that our acts proceed from ourselves . . . by virtue of which everyone must recognize them as *his* actions' (*FW/TFP*, pp. 95–6/106). My actions are those acts that issue from my innermost nature, my character, which is both inborn and unchanging throughout my life. Schopenhauer, drawing on Kant's doctrine, identifies the ultimate source of an individual's nature as the intelligible character, which is distinct from what we know of a person's character and what he himself knows of it, as it is displayed in his thoughts and actions in the course of his life: his empirical character. A person's existence in time is a manifestation to a definite degree of the will as thing-in-itself, an act of will outside time (*WWR* I, p. 289). This is his intelligible character, the source of the phenomenal individual's moral freedom. For, since it is given outside time, it is not subject to the causal necessity that reigns in the phenomenal realm. Hence there is a sense in which it can be said that my intelligible character could have been other than it is, since there was no sufficient reason for its having taken the form that it did. So it makes sense to say that I could have had a different character from the one I do have; and even though, given my character, I could not have done otherwise in the situation that I found myself, I might have acted differently had my character been different. It is the thought of this possibility, Schopenhauer suggests, which underpins and makes intelligible our sense of responsibility for, and our feelings of guilt over, our actions.

As well as being inborn, human character is constant: we cannot change our nature – a person of bad character will always tend to act badly. This does not imply that a person's behaviour may never be surprising, for our knowledge of a person's (empirical) character is derived piecemeal at different times and in different circumstances. And people change their behaviour in the light of their knowledge of their circumstances. It is the capacity for the increasing correction and enlargement of knowledge that, Schopenhauer argues, allows for the possibility of virtuous action.

But, he stresses, the knowledge which leads to virtue is not abstract knowledge communicable in words, neither the dogmas of priests and moralists, nor the formulas, principles and arguments of philosophers: such knowledge does not affect the goodness of disposition (*WWR* I, p. 368). As Seneca, the teacher of Nero, had said, and Schopenhauer liked to quote, '*Velle non discitur*' (willing cannot be taught). Rather, the knowledge in question is 'direct and intuitive' and must 'dawn on each of us' (*WWR* I, p. 370).

According to Schopenhauer, the egoist and the malicious person act in ignorance, for, even though they may not have articulated it to themselves, they act as though their distinctness from other human beings is significant – they see others as enemies who have to be outwitted or harmed. The compassionate person, on the other hand, realizes the truth communicated in Schopenhauer's philosophy without necessarily hearing the propositions or studying the arguments: that the differences between people are mere appearance, and that in reality all people, all living things, are essentially the same. The compassionate person recognizes his own inner being in others; he sees others as 'I once more' rather than 'not-I' (*BM/TFP*, pp. 211/254). In light of this understanding, compassionate people are capable of disinterested love and of acting selflessly towards others. Love is compassion, Schopenhauer maintains (*WWR* I, p. 374), conscious of the seeming paradox, since love as ordinarily understood in sexual relationships is selfish and domineering.

This account does not seem at first sight to capture the real character of compassionate action. Acting lovingly towards others for the reason that I see *myself* in them looks merely to be an enlarged egoism: if I feel the other's pain as my own, then my acting to relieve his pain is a way of relieving my own pain. Schopenhauer is alive to this problem and makes use of the resources of the German concept of sympathy – *Mitleid*, literally 'feeling with' – to clarify his position.

at every moment we remain clearly conscious that *he* is the sufferer, not *we*; and it is precisely in *his* person, not in ours, that we feel the suffering, to our grief and sorrow. We suffer *with* him and hence *in* him; we feel his pain as *his*, and do not imagine it as ours. In fact, the happier our state, and hence the more the consciousness of it is contrasted with the other man's fate, the more susceptible we are to compassion. (*BM/TFP*, pp. 147/203)

This passage, which combines philosophical acumen with psychological insight, brings out the fact that compassion bridges rather than abolishes the separateness of people from one another. The natural egoistic view of the world motivating self-interested action is replaced by compassion when someone no longer sees others as absolutely distinct from himself, when the distinctness strikes them as insignificant. Schopenhauer understands that the development of compassion for others can be the beginning of a process of transformation in which a person's sense of the distinctness of individuals progressively weakens as his realization of the illusoriness of phenomenal things deepens. The Veil of Māyā gradually thins or lifts; his old character is suppressed, rather than changed, as knowledge of the thing-in-itself replaces phenomenal knowledge; he withdraws from life and gives up willing. This is what Schopenhauer characterizes as the path to salvation, which leads to the eventual denial of the will-to-live and to escape from the world. While he concedes that this process is mysterious, he is just as convinced of its genuineness as he is of the existence of compassion.

It is a mystery to students of Schopenhauer how a man can exhibit such insight into the nature of compassion and virtuous action and yet display so little of them in his own relationships with people. His response to the disparity between life and work was to assert that it 'as little necessary for the saint to be a philosopher as for the philosopher to be a saint' (*WWR* I, p. 383). The understanding of life which, as a philosopher, Schopenhauer was able to present in abstract theories and propositions never took the form of an immediate, intuitive awareness that would have transformed his inner disposition and responses to people. Aside from his sympathy for animal suffering, his compassion was directed towards the species of humanity rather than to individuals. He could not live the philosophy of life that he articulated.

7

The Sage of Frankfurt

'Doomsday on Hegelian Philosophy' was the title of a review of *Two Fundamental Problems of Ethics* in May 1841 which characterized Schopenhauer as the greatest philosopher of the age. Though this accolade appeared in a literary periodical, *The Pilot*, rather than an academic journal,[1] the anonymous author was clearly abreast of current thinking within the groves of academe. The previous year the newly crowned King of Prussia, Friedrich Wilhelm IV, had called the 65-year-old Schelling to Berlin, the headquarters of the Hegelians, to put an end to Hegelianism, which had already split into left- and right-wing factions since Hegel's death. In spite of his reputation as one of the architects, along with Fichte and Hegel, of German Idealism, Schelling arrived in Berlin as the prophet of a new era. When he delivered his lectures in August 1841 his audience – which was too big for the largest hall in the University – comprised not just professors and academics but statesman and young intellectuals such as Mikhail Bakunin, Friedrich Engels and, on a visit from Denmark, Søren Kierkegaard. The moment was symbolic of the immense changes, political, social and intellectual, that were gradually working through the Germanic kingdoms, and which in due course would make it possible for Schopenhauer's philosophy to be recognized and celebrated.

The anonymous review may have anticipated by many years Schopenhauer's annunciation as a great philosopher, but it did address itself to the appropriate audience. While academic reviews

Julius Frauenstädt, friend and disciple of Schopenhauer.

of *The Two Fundamental Problems of Ethics* and *On the Will in Nature* were dismissive, the few enthusiastic readers of Schopenhauer at this time came, for the most part, from the professional middle class outside the universities. Judges and lawyers, together with a private scholar, constituted the vanguard of admirers with whom he was in contact in the late 1830s and '40s; a little later, there was added a teacher of English, a doctor, a newspaper editor and a bank employee. Schopenhauer playfully spoke of them as his Apostles, though their number never reached the canonical twelve. The 'primary evangelist', as Schopenhauer dubbed him, was Judge Friedrich Dorguth from Magdeburg who at the age of 62 had written a critique of Hegelianism, a copy of which he sent to Feuerbach, before he was stimulated by reading *On the Will in*

Nature into contacting Schopenhauer in 1836. Julius Frauenstädt, whom Schopenhauer regarded as his 'arch-evangelist', had become disenchanted with the Hegelian philosophy he studied at the University of Berlin and then written about Feuerbach's philosophy before turning to Schopenhauer. He became a friend and advisor to Schopenhauer after their meeting in 1847, as well as a tireless publicist of his philosophy.

For the early followers, acquaintance with Schopenhauer's philosophy came through the first edition of *The World as Will and Representation*. But by 1841, Schopenhauer was immersed in preparing the second edition. His conception of it was ambitious, not to say extravagant. The text of the first edition was to remain unchanged, apart from some minor clarifications and the rewriting of the Appendix on Kant's philosophy in the light of his discovery of the first edition of the first *Critique*. Though his fundamental views had not changed since 1818, he wanted in the second edition to work through all the parts of his philosophy more thoroughly in a series of essays, arranged according to the fourfold division of the original presentation. In short, the second edition would not be a correction of the first but an enlargement, requiring a second volume as big again as the first. Schopenhauer saw the two volumes as complementary to one another. The first would display 'the fire of youth and the energy of original conception', whereas the second would embody the maturity of a long and industrious life.

Sharp-witted persuasion was required to overcome his publisher's reluctance to accept the two volumes, but in March 1844 the second edition of *The World as Will and Representation* was published by Brockhaus. In the short run, its fate was similar to that of the first, with few sales and even fewer reviews. The addition of the supplementary essays made little difference to the familiar line already taken by reviewers of Schopenhauer's work. In fact, however, in Essay 18 he directly confronted, and arguably changed his position on, the most fundamental doctrine of his philosophy, the identification of the thing-in-itself with will. First-time readers of volume I of *The World as Will and Representation* tend to think that Schopenhauer argues that our immediate knowledge of willing provides access to the thing-in-itself and thus enables us to realize its nature as will (see *WWR* I, pp. 100, 112). The problem here was stated succinctly in a manuscript note Schopenhauer made at Mannheim in the summer of 1824 while recovering from illness. '*To know the thing-in-itself* – is a contradiction because all knowledge is *representation*, but thing-in-itself means the thing in so far as it is *not* representation' (*MR* III, p. 195).

In the supplementary essay entitled, 'On the Possibility of Knowing the Thing-in-Itself' (*WWR* II, pp. 191–200), Schopenhauer acknowledged that, since what is known in willing is individual acts, particular actions, which take place at distinct times (*WWR* II, p. 107), and time is a form of representation, what is known in willing cannot be the thing-in-itself. Nevertheless, he insists that because this inner knowledge of willing is free of the forms of space and causality, the thing-in-itself has, as it were, cast off some of its veils. 'Accordingly, the act of will is indeed only the nearest and clearest *phenomenon* of the thing-in-itself' (*WWR* II, p. 197). That is to say, in the experience of willing we know the thing-in-itself more immediately and intimately than we do in any other experience and hence we can be confident in thinking of the inner nature of everything as will. But to make this claim, Schopenhauer has to admit that 'the thing-in-itself . . . may have, entirely outside all possible phenomenon, determinations, qualities, and modes of existence which for us are absolutely unknowable and incomprehensible' (*WWR* II, p. 198). Here Schopenhauer seems to have retreated to the Kantian orthodoxy from which his philosophy had supposedly escaped.

Despite Schopenhauer's effort to clarify his views, the 'disciples' continued to press him on the topic of will and thing-in-itself, and when Frauenstädt had the temerity to suggest that, like Kant,

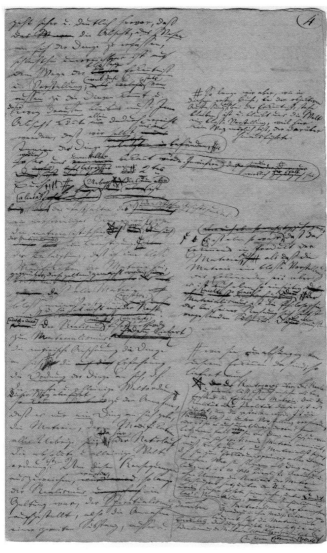

A page of the manuscript of the radically extended second edition of *The World as Will and Representation*, published in 1844.

Schopenhauer should have refrained from saying anything about the thing-in-itself, he replied robustly.

> Then I could have immediately thrown my whole philosophy out of the window. It is precisely my great discovery that Kant's thing-in-itself is that which we find in self-consciousness as the will . . . But this will is thing-in-itself merely in relation to appearance . . . (*GB*, p. 288).[2]

In a subsequent letter, he confirmed his adherence to Kantianism by telling Frauenstädt that he did not know what the thing-in-itself is outside of its relation to appearance and that to attempt to speak of it would be to enter the cloud-cuckoo land where the God of the Jews and the Absolute of Hegel sit (*GB*, pp. 290–91). What these letters show is that for the mature Schopenhauer the question 'Can we know the thing-in-itself?', is ambivalent between 'Can we know the thing-in-itself in its relation to appearance?' and 'Can we know the thing-in-itself outside its relation to appearance?' To the latter question, as a sincere Kantian, Schopenhauer's answer is 'No'. To the former, his answer is 'Yes', for the cornerstone of Schopenhauerianism is that the thing-in-itself reveals itself in appearance as will; the will to life.[3]

The doctrine of life in the grip of the will underlies the pessimistic view of the world that Schopenhauer develops further in the supplementary essay on the vanity and suffering of life (*WWR* II, pp. 573–88). The pessimism of Schopenhauer's philosophy is not that, or not merely that, of someone who is inclined to dwell on only the bad things in life or who emphasizes the bad over the good. Certainly, he was of that temperament. But the pessimism of his philosophy has deeper roots than personal psychology. It derives from the metaphysics of the world as will, of the view of life as the manifestation of nothing more than a blind, endless striving which makes suffering inevitable. For suffering is intrinsic to the structure of individual consciousness, instantiating the will's striving in number-less needs and wants propelling us into action to fulfil them. All willing, Schopenhauer points out, begins with 'need, lack, and hence pain' (*WWR* I, p. 312), obviously so with respect to the lack of food and water but also true of more refined desires for fashionable clothes or the solution to a scientific problem. Obstacles that frustrate the fulfilment of desires serve only to aggravate their intensity. Fulfilment does bring satisfaction, though this is soon replaced by new desires demanding action. Even were we to satisfy most desires, we would not achieve happiness, for satiety itself would give rise to a new form of suffering: 'dreariness, emptiness, and boredom follow, the struggle against which is just as painful as that against want' (*WWR* I, p. 314).

Of course, Schopenhauer does not think that life is nothing but misery. On the contrary, what history shows is that human life everywhere provides material for both tragedy and comedy. But since he understands pleasure to be essentially the absence of pain, it follows that the reality of pain must always outweigh pleasure. Ultimately, all lives are unhappy, though each is unhappy in its own way. This truth is expressed allegorically in the Old Testament myth of the Fall of man (*WWR* II, p. 580) and the Christian view of life as a vale of tears. However, this doctrine is obscured by what he regarded as the optimism of Jewish theology. Schopenhauer reserved his bitterest scorn for theologians and philosophers who proclaim that life is a blessing or that all is for the good. Optimism, when it is not merely 'thoughtless talk', is wicked, 'a bitter mockery of the unspeakable sufferings of mankind' (*WWR* I, p. 326). In response to Leibniz's notorious doctrine that this is the best of all possible worlds, Schopenhauer dramatically offered to prove that this is the *worst* of all possible worlds (*WWR* II, p. 583). It is possible to imagine conditions to be worse than they currently are; what he denies is that such a world would be capable of continuing to exist, for the wors-ening conditions would render life either impossible or intolerable.

The world as it is permits the maximum degree of suffering compatible with its continued existence. Throughout his work, he drew on his own observations of human behaviour as well as historical sources to document what he regarded as the 'infinite pain which everywhere abounds in the world and springs from the want and misery essential to life' (*PP* II, p. 291). And it was the sixth-century BC Greek poet Theognis whose expression of ancient wisdom provided Schopenhauer with the keenest statement of his pessimism: 'Not to be born is the best for man.'[4]

Schopenhauer claimed that an outcry had been raised against 'the melancholy and cheerless nature' of his philosophy (*WWR* II, p. 580). Certainly, at the time of the first and of the second edition of *The World as Will and Representation*, it was in conflict with the progressive movements within Germany. The disappointment and disillusion that followed the crushing defeat of the revolutionary activity of 1848–9 made Schopenhauer's pessimism more palatable to some, the most notable of whom was the composer Richard Wagner. Born in 1813, he had grown up in the period during which the monarchies of the German Confederation had succeeded in repressing the sporadic attempts by workers and intellectuals to achieve social and political reforms, as had occurred at the Hamburger Fest of 1832. And like many others, Wagner had been swept up in the excitement ignited by the news from France in February 1848 that the French monarchy had been overthrown. Disturbances subsequently broke out in many European cities, most seriously in Vienna, which led to the fall of Prince Metternich, the Austrian architect of the Confederation, and in Berlin, where the monarchy was sufficiently panicked to make concessions to the demands of the protesters. Alarmed by these developments and by the fighting in Frankfurt, Schopenhauer took stock of his possessions, cut back on his book orders and made economies in his way of living. As he reported to Frauenstädt, 'if a storm threatens, one draws in all sails' (*GB*, p. 231).

Schopenhauer was aware of the dreadful suffering of factory workers (*WWR* II, p. 578), but his sympathy for their plight did not extend to support for their cause. His general position was that efforts to banish suffering achieve nothing more than a change in its form (*WWR* I, p. 315) and that the workers' hopes of happiness were merely misconceived optimism fuelled by shallow intellectuals. The assertion that the workers had nothing to lose but their chains, made by Marx and Engels in *The Communist Manifesto*, published in London at the beginning of 1848, he would have regarded as an expression of ignorance of the real nature of the world. Democracy, he thought in common with Plato, would allow the greater numbers of inferior minds in a republic to overwhelm those of superior intellect who were better able to rule. The latter would be more likely to have preferment under a hereditary monarchy in which the monarch, by being so far above all others in power, wealth and security, would have no other interest except that of ruling for the good of his subjects (*WWR* II, p. 595; *PP* II, pp. 254–5).

To Schopenhauer's relief, the gathering political storm was decisively defused in September 1848. There was a terrifying outbreak of violence in Frankfurt on 18 September directed against the All-German Assembly in the St Paul's Church by radical workers who had lost patience with the impotence of the middle-class 'talking-shop'. Two Assembly representatives were mauled to death by the mob, while the remainder had to be rescued by Prussian and Austrian troops. From his apartment at 17 Schöne Aussicht, Schopenhauer saw what he called 'a large rabble armed with pitchforks, poles and a few rifles, with a red flag carried ahead of it' crossing the bridge into the city. He later described to the police that a rifleman fired into the roadway 'with the greatest calm and deliberation'.[5] He heard hammering on his door, assumed it was 'the sovereign *canaille*' and rushed to bar the door, but his maidservant realized it was the Austrians. Schopenhauer immediately showed the blue-trousered soldiers to a suitable vantage point at his windows from which they could fire on the protesters. They later decided to move to the house next door and Schopenhauer lent the commanding officer his 'big, double opera glasses' so that he could get a better view of 'the rabble behind the barricade' (*GB*, p. 234). When calm was restored to the city, Schopenhauer shocked his fellow-diners at the *Englischer Hof*, conservative aristocratic officers, with the vehemence of his denunciation of one of the leaders of the mob as well as with his vociferous praise for 'the noble Prince Windischgrätz' who had helped put down the rebellion. Wagner's anarchist friend, Bakunin, was sentenced to death for his role in the uprising in Dresden in May 1849, though this was commuted to life imprisonment, whereas Wagner himself, who had also manned the barricades, was fortunate to escape to Switzerland where a few years later his view of the world was revolutionized by his reading of Schopenhauer's philosophy. Ironically, the author of that philosophy, under the terms of his will of 1852, left the bulk of his estate to the benefit of the wounded Prussian soldiers, and the relatives of those who had been killed, for their part in restoring legal order in Germany during the years 1848 and 1849.

In Bonn on 20 August 1849 Adele dictated to her 'intimate friend', Sibylle Mertens-Schaaffhausen, a last letter to her brother. She expressed her wholehearted thanks for his friendship of recent months, having only enough strength to sign the letter 'your faithful sister'.[6] Adele had been seriously ill for a number of years and Schopenhauer had met her in Frankfurt a few months earlier when she, accompanied by Mertens-Schaaffhausen, was making her valedictory visits to friends around Germany. In his prompt reply, Schopenhauer regretted that she should concern herself with 'all sorts of trivial, worldly and hopefully superfluous' matters on her sickbed, and hoped that she would not 'change lives, as we Buddhists call it' but that heaven would strengthen and preserve her (*GB*, p. 236).[7] Mertens-Schaaffhausen read the letter to Adele the day before she died on 25 August. Of the two people closest to Adele, it was Sibylle Mertens-Schaaffhausen, rather than Schopenhauer, who was most affected by her death. The wife of a banker, she had known Adele during the Weimar days, and had been of assistance to her and her mother when they were in financial difficulty. They had been living together since 1842, and it was Mertens-Schaaffhausen who nursed Adele through her long illness, made all the funeral arrangements and erected a monument to mark her grave. Schopenhauer did not attend the funeral. As well as receiving some family heirlooms, Schopenhauer benefited financially from Adele's death, but what gave him greatest pleasure were his father's notebooks of their European tour. Adele was the person who had known him most intimately, and the one who had seen through his harsh judgements of humanity to the anguish that drove him to seek understanding of the suffering in the world. She thought of him, she said, as 'a holy thinker'.[8]

In the late 1840s Schopenhauer determined to make a last effort to reach out beyond his small but growing group of disciples to a wider audience. He put together a large collection of essays which, divided into two volumes, was even longer than the two volumes of the second edition of *The World as Will and Representation.* Despite its forbidding title, *Parerga und Paralipomena* – literally 'supplements and omissions' – the book was intended to have a broad appeal to educated readers. This was due as much to the style as to the content. While there were some discussions of the details of his system, the bulk of the book was accessible to those who were not familiar with his philosophy. He dealt with a wide range of subjects of general intellectual interest: some explicitly philosophical, such as the history and the methodology of philosophy; and some not, such as Sanskrit literature, reading and education. Moreover, his presentation was much more informal than that of earlier books: the tone was that of someone speaking seriously, but with wry scepticism, after long reflection on the problems of living. He even added as a coda a number of poems written at different times in his life. By far the longest section of the book was entitled 'Aphorisms on the Wisdom of Life'. In it, pointedly setting aside the pessimism of his principal works, he considered 'the art of getting through life as pleasantly and successfully as possible' and provided 'instructions on how to have a happy existence' (*PP* I, p. 313). Here Schopenhauer's dazzling literary gifts came together with his remarkable erudition to achieve a heady mixture of worldly wisdom and acerbic wit. There was also much in *Parerga und Paralipomena* that was endearingly eccentric, such as the outbursts against the vogue for long beards (I, p. 175) and against mindless noise-making by whistlers, whip-crackers, door-slammers and those who let dogs bark (II, pp. 643–4).

In his attempts to get Brockhaus to accept the *Parerga* for publication, Schopenhauer claimed that it would be his last book and that it would be popular, for he had written a 'philosophy for the world' (*GB*, p. 244). But Brockhaus had lost patience with their loss-making philosopher. Two other publishers rejected Schopenhauer's proposal before his 'worthy Apostle', Frauenstädt, came to his assistance and made an arrangement with a Berlin publisher who delivered *Parerga und Paralipomena* to the world towards the end of 1851. From December onwards, a steady stream of appreciative reviews began to appear in literary journals around Germany, first anonymous and then signed articles, including three from Schopenhauer's disciples. Then, in April 1852, an unsigned review appeared in the London journal *The Westminster Review*, the first notice of any of Schopenhauer's works outside Germany. At that time, *The Westminster Review* was edited by Mary Ann Evans, who later became famous as the novelist George Eliot. She was a keen student of German intellectual life and had translated into English Strauss's *The Life of Jesus, Critically Examined* (1846); she was also soon to translate Feuerbach's *The Essence of Christianity* (1854). The following year she gave the author, critic and translator of Goethe John Oxenford, who had written the original review of *Parerga*

und Paralipomena, the opportunity to write at length about
Schopenhauer's philosophy in an article entitled 'Iconoclasm in
German Philosophy'.[9] In twenty pages Oxenford provided the first
comprehensive account of Schopenhauer's philosophy ever to be
published. Relating Schopenhauer's ideas to those of Kant and
Berkeley, he identified him as an original and distinctive voice in
modern German thought, a voice whose clarity, directness and
intelligibility contrasted markedly with the vague convolutions
of the schools of Hegel and Schelling. While Oxenford evidently
delighted in Schopenhauer's style, he was nonetheless distressed
by his pessimism, 'the most disheartening, the most repulsive,
the most opposed to the aspirations of the present world, that the
most ardent of Job's comforters could concoct'.[10] Schopenhauer
was greatly pleased by the article, and was especially impressed
with Oxenford's translations of a number of passages from *The
Fourfold Root* and *The World as Will and Representation*, though he
was not totally satisfied, finding the account of his ethical views
unsatisfactory and disputing Oxenford's characterization of him
as the misanthropic sage of Frankfurt. Later in 1853 a translation of
Oxenford's article appeared in *Vossiche Zeitung*, a Berlin newspaper
edited by one of Schopenhauer's more recent disciples, E. O. Linder.
This was the publication which became the catalyst for Schopenhauer's rise to fame throughout Germany and Europe.

During 1852–3 there were signs that the passive resistance to
Schopenhauer's work among the professors of philosophy was
gradually crumbling. Academics at Heidelberg, Tübingen and
Halle wrote extensively about Schopenhauer, while successive
editions of the journal *Zeitschrift für Philosophie und philosophische
Kritik* carried ever more discussions of his work.[11] 'Their Casper
Hauser . . . has escaped', was how Schopenhauer gleefully put it in
the second edition of *On the Will in Nature* in 1854, 'and he is running
around the world' (p. 5).[12] However, his liberator had not been the
professors but the public; that is, the educated middle-class public

Johann Valentin Albert, *Schopenhauer* (aged 64), 1852, daguerreotype.

epitomized by Schopenhauer's disciples. This class had grown
steadily in the wake of the urbanization and industrialization of
the German states in the previous twenty years and there had been
an expansion of publishing and journalism to cater for its tastes,
witnessed by the fact that the number of bookshops in the principal
cities had doubled between 1831 and 1855.[13] The manifest literary
merits of Schopenhauer's writing, especially the essays of *Parerga
und Paralipomena*, meant that his philosophy was accessible to non-
specialized readers in a way that Hegel, Schelling and Fichte were

not. Moreover, his rejection of grand political theorizing and scorn for theories of history proclaiming the triumph of reason chimed with the mood of a public chastened by the events of 1848–9 and by the the restoration of the French monarchy under Napoleon III in 1852. His was a philosophy, too, that was grounded in immediate experience familiar to all, while at the same time acknowledging the importance of the empirical sciences in which Germany was on the way to becoming a world-leader. Indeed, on the strength of his growing popularity, Schopenhauer was able to arrange in 1854 the second editions of *On the Will in Nature* and *On Vision and Colours*, his two works dealing most explicitly with scientific theory.

The verdict of Marx and Engels, and other political activists, on Schopenhauer's appeal to the bourgeoisie was that he produced 'vapid reflections . . . fashioned to fit the philistines'.[14] But Schopenhauer's philosophy attracted then, and long continued to attract, the attention of artists, in part because of the high value Schopenhauer attached to art and music and, in consequence, the high status he assigned to artistic genius. However, it was not his view of the arts that was ultimately responsible for the deep impression that Schopenhauer made on Richard Wagner, but the philosophy of pessimism and the renunciation of life. Wagner first encountered *The World as Will and Representation* in the autumn of 1854 during his exile in Switzerland, where he had fled to escape imprisonment after the crushing of the uprising in Dresden in 1849. For Wagner, who had previously taken an interest in Hegel and Feuerbach, Schopenhauer came as a revelation: 'like a gift from heaven', as he put it in a letter to Liszt.[15] By the following summer he had read *The World as Will and Representation* four times. Schopenhauer, he told Liszt, was 'the greatest philosopher since Kant . . . What charlatans all these Hegels etc. are beside him!' He regarded Schopenhauer's principal idea to be 'the final denial of the will to live'. At the time of his first reading of *The World as Will and Representation*, Wagner was struggling with his conception of the

conclusion to his tetralogy, *The Ring of the Niebelung*. He had thought
that the work would have a hopeful political conclusion in which a
just world would be achieved through the elimination of injustice,
but on reading Schopenhauer he realized that all along he had been
working against his deepest instincts as an artist.[16] Even though
Wagner had constructed a philosophy of Hellenic Optimism in
prose works such as *Opera and Drama*, the evidence of his operas
The Flying Dutchman, *Tannhäuser* and *Lohengrin* showed that he
was an artist of tragedy, of negation of the will and the renunciation
of life. Wagner reworked the ending of *The Ring* – 'only now did
I understand my own Wotan'[17] – and abandoned his theory that
music in opera is a means to the realization of the truth enshrined
in the drama in favour of Schopenhauer's: that it is in and through
the music that the deepest truths are revealed.[18]

In December 1854 Wagner sent to Schoenhauer a copy of *The
Ring* poem in a luxurious format, without a covering letter, but
with the dedication 'With reverence and gratitude'. Schopenhauer
was never to realize the significance of these words for Wagner, who
was undoubtedly the greatest artist to acknowledge Schopenhauer's
genius in his lifetime and whose increasingly influential advocacy
played a major role in establishing his reputation throughout Europe.
Wagner's name was not unknown to Schopenhauer. Earlier in the
year he had attended a performance of *The Flying Dutchman* and
had given his approval to an article in a Berlin newspaper in which
the critic Karl Kossack had employed quotations from Schopenhauer
to attack Wagner's operas and his theory of the 'total work of art'
(*Gesamtkunstwerk*). When he received a visit from one of Wagner's
friends in the spring of 1855 bearing greetings from Wagner,
Schopenhauer asked him to convey his thanks for the gift of *The
Ring* poem, adding the advice that Wagner should give up music –
'His genius is greater as a poet. I, Schopenhauer, remain faithful
to Rossini and Mozart' (*G*, p. 199–200).[19] He had read Wagner's
poem with considerable care, as is manifest in his many annotations

to the manuscript. Like a crusty old professor, he snorted over Wagner's imaginative neologisms and grammatical improprieties – 'The gentleman seems to think the language is his serf' – and like any respectable member of the bourgeoisie he was shocked by the incest between Siegmund and Sieglinde in *Die Walküre*, though many of the comments display his gift for sarcasm – 'Wotan under the slipper!', he writes at the point where the chief of the gods is obliged to bow to his wife's will – and some markings of the text are indicative, perhaps, of his approval of the verse.[20] Wagner was disappointed to receive no direct communication from Schopenhauer about *The Ring* poem or about the libretto for *Tristan and Isolde*, which he sent Schopenhauer in 1859. He thought of visiting Schopenhauer in Frankfurt in 1860, yet when the time came he found he could not bring himself to meet his hero; just as Schopenhauer, too, had been unable to bring himself to speak to Byron in 1819 or to Rossini when he visited Frankfurt in 1856 (*G*, pp. 220–21). Nonetheless, Wagner's admiration and gratitude for Schopenhauer's philosophy never waned but sustained him throughout the rest of his turbulent life.

Wagner was just one of the numerous enthusiastic readers who were drawn to Schopenhauer's philosophy in the wake of the publicity given to it by Oxenford's article. Frauenstädt reproduced it in his *Letters on the Schopenhauerian Philosophy*, published in 1854, the first book-length examination of Schopenhauer's thought, whose committed advocacy helped fan the flames of Schopenhauer's fame. In a relatively short time Schopenhauer became, bizarre as it seems, a celebrity; and not just a local celebrity in Frankfurt. The tenor of his life changed. Though he maintained his daily routine, visitors would join him at his home prior to lunch or accompany him on his afternoon walk with his poodle. 'Today there came two Russians, two Swedes, and two ladies', he reported.[21] When he took lunch at the *Englischer Hof*, there would be people sitting at tables just for the opportunity of observing him. Notes were made,

Johann Jacob Seib, *Schopenhauer* (aged 67), 1855, daguerreotype.

and circulated, of his conversations, actions and appearance. Schopenhauer was hungry to learn of any published reference to himself, large or small, a hunger that the disciples were enjoined to feed with cuttings and reports from newspapers and journals throughout Germany. He sat for his portrait more than once; he was photographed by means of the daguerrotype; a bust was made by a young Berlin sculptor, Elizabeth Ney, whose intelligence and artistry won over the old misogynist. And like any celebrity, he attracted some strange devotees, such as the landowner who purchased an oil portrait by Lunteschütz and displayed it like an icon above a shelf of Schopenhauer's works in a purpose-built house, and the gentleman in Bohemia who placed a fresh wreath on his portrait every day. When the dramatist Friedrich Hebbel visited him in May 1857, Schopenhauer told him he felt like the lamplighter in the theatre who, when the house lights go down and the curtain rises, is still busy with the footlights and has to hurriedly scamper into the wings; 'just so am I on stage for the tragic farce, called the world, while the comedy of my fame is beginning' (*G*, p. 306).

In March 1856, replying to Frauenstädt's congratulations on his 68th birthday, Schopenhauer declared himself to be in excellent health, fit enough to swim in the river Main every summer, and with no ailments apart from defective hearing. His left ear, which he had relied on since the illness of 1823 had rendered his right almost deaf, was beginning to fail, making it difficult for him to enjoy the theatre unless it was loud, as in farces and operas (*GB*, p. 386). Apart from a fall in the winter of 1857 when he injured his forehead while taking his usual vigorous evening walk, an event reported in the Frankfurt newspapers, he maintained his generally good health until the very end of his life. In 1859, anxious about escape in case of fire, he moved from his apartment at 17 Schöne Aussicht, where he had lived since 1843, to the ground-floor apartment at number 16.

The nature of death was an aspect of the riddle of existence that Schopenhauer had wanted his philosophy to resolve, for he recognized that death is generally regarded as the greatest of all evils, giving rise to the greatest anxiety (*WWR* II, p. 465). Indeed, he thought that if it were not for death, there would be very little philosophy or religion (*WWR* II, p. 463). And since he wanted his philosophy to be of use to people, he set out to show that death is not something to be feared. But it would not suffice to characterize death simply as a refuge or relief from the miseries of life, for most people would be prepared to suffer the most fearful pain in order to avoid a quick and easy death.

The weariest and most loathèd worldly life
That age, ache, penury, and imprisonment
Can lay on nature is a paradise
To what we fear of death.[22]

Yet instinctive fear can to some extent be allayed by arguments, such as those espoused by the ancient philosophers. Schopenhauer followed Epicurus in thinking that non-existence is something it is not rational to fear, for it cannot be experienced: just as we are undisturbed by the fact of our non-existence prior to birth, so our non-existence after death is equally unthreatening.[23] Religions that hold out the prospect of personal immortality Schopenhauer regarded as both confused and immoral: confused in that they rely upon the action of a deity to create something, life, out of nothing, which he regarded as strictly impossible; and immoral in that they appeal to the basest egoism as motivation for the achievement of posthumous happiness. He was prepared to argue for immortality as a part of nature, the endless cycle of living and dying, manifesting the unchanging will to life. To be anxious about death is to over-look the real nature of human identity. According to Schopenhauer's idealism, the distinct personality living at a certain time and place is not absolutely real, but mere appearance in contrast to the reality of the thing-in-itself, the will. Time itself is ideal, the necessary form of phenomena; the thing-in-itself is timeless. The temporal character of our existence – being born at a certain time, living for a specific length of time, dying at a later time – is unreal, illusory, whereas our real nature as will is outside time, unchanging and changeless. Schopenhauer dramatically presents this insight with an image of the sun appearing to fall into night and rise at dawn when it is actually burning continuously. 'If, therefore, a person fears death as his annihilation, it is just as if he were to think that the sun can lament in the evening and say: "Woe is me! I am going down into eternal night"' (*WWR* I, p. 280).

However, if, as Schopenhauer maintains, life is full of misery and what is lost in death is of no importance, then it is surely rational to commit suicide. He rejected this reasoning, regarding suicide as a vain and foolish action (*WWR* I, p. 281), though never as morally wrong. Indeed, with the memory of his father's suicide, he was scathing in his attack on the attitude of the conventional church and legal system which branded suicides as criminals (*PP* II, pp. 306–11). Suicide was a mistake rather than a crime. Suicide cannot achieve salvation, because suicide is an affirmation of the will to live, whereas salvation requires denial of the will. Paradoxical as it seems to regard the act of self-destruction as an affirmation rather than a denial of the will to live, Schopenhauer here has a profound insight into the character of suicide undertaken in order to escape suffering, whether it be bodily pain or disgrace and humiliation. Were his suffering somehow to evaporate, the would-be suicide would be happy to resume his life. 'The suicide wills life, and is dissatisfied merely with the conditions on which it has come to him' (*WWR* I, p. 398), whereas denial of the will to live consists essentially in 'the fact that the pleasures of life, not its sorrows, are shunned'. What is more, the suicide's wilful act denies him the opportunity his suffering provides: to lead him to the denial of the will and so to salvation. 'The suicide is like a sick man who, after the beginning of a painful operation that could completely cure him, will not allow it to be completed, but prefers to retain his illness' (*WWR* I, p. 399).

Schopenhauer's notion of denial of the will is not without difficulties, as he himself recognized (*WWR* I, p. 402f.). If phenomenal individuals are no more than manifestations of the will-to-live, then how is it possible for them to deny the will? It is certainly an outright contradiction to speak of willing the denial of the will. Schopenhauer regards the quieting of the will as something which comes over a person, 'as if flying in from without' (*WWR* I, p. 404). Just as someone may suddenly see the figure in a puzzle-picture, so it may dawn on them that the phenomenal world of space and time is illusory, unreal, and that the life of struggle and strife is futile. The quieting of the will is a manifestation of freedom; indeed, it is the only direct expression in phenomenal life of the freedom of the will. As a person's entry into life is unconditioned act of will, and to that extent arbitrary, so a person's resignation from life is unconditioned, and to that extent unpredictable. It is comparable to what in Christianity is called the effect of grace descending from God (*wwr* I, p. 403), and its effect is not merely a change in one's character but a suppression of one's old character: one is, as it were, born again.

While knowledge, the knowledge that pierces the Veil of Māyā and quiets the will, is the high road to salvation, Schopenhauer recognizes an alternative route via extreme suffering in which a person's will to live is broken through pain, degradation or despair. It is this latter route that, by deliberately ending his life, the suicide fails to take. Either way, the individual renounces the world. The life of such a person will be marked by asceticism and chastity, in which the demands of the body will be resisted. It is a way of life, Schopenhauer points out, that is exemplified in the lives of the Christian saints and of the holy men of the Hindus and Buddhists (*wwr* I, p. 383). The blissful states enjoyed by people who have denied the will, and which are described in the mystical writings of these religions, is made intelligible through Schopenhauer's negative theory of pleasure, for by eliminating desire such people thereby eliminate suffering and enjoy the peace of mind hinted at in our experiences of art. As Schopenhauer puts it in one of his most beautiful passages,

> Nothing can distress or alarm him any more; nothing can any longer move him; for he has cut all the thousand threads of willing which hold us bound to the world, and which as craving, fear, envy, and anger drag us here and there in constant pain.

He now looks back calmly and with a smile on the phantas-
magoria of this world which was once able to move and agonize
his mind, but now stands before him as indifferently as chess-
men at the end of a game, or as fancy dress cast off in the
morning, the form and figure of which taunted and disquieted
us on the carnival night. Life and its forms merely float before
him as a fleeting phenomenon, as a light morning dream to one
half-awake, through which reality already shines, and which can
no longer deceive; and, like this morning dream, they too finally
vanish without any violent transition. (*WWR* I, pp. 390–91).

The death of the person who has practised denial of the will is
dramatically different from that of those who continue to affirm
life. Not only is there no 'violent transition', it is also without
fear and grief; and, even more significantly, 'it is not merely the
phenomenon, as in the case of others, that comes to an end with
death, but the inner being itself is abolished' (*WWR* I, p. 382). The
clear implication of this is that the inner being of those who affirm
life is not abolished at death. Schopenhauer did not enlarge on the
point in the first edition of *The World as Will and Representation* but
he did do so in the second edition, especially in the supplementary
essay 41, 'On Death and Its Relation to the Indestructibility of Our
Inner Nature' (*WWR* II, pp. 463–509), which betrays the influence
of his further researches into the doctrines of the ancient Indian
religions. They, like all religions, present philosophical truths
about life and the world in metaphorical and pictorial form so that
members of the wider population can better understand them than
when they are elaborated in systems of philosophy. He regarded
the Indian doctrine of the cycle of rebirth as a mythological version
of his own philosophy of eternal justice and denial of the will.
The person who affirms life is like someone who has led a life of
wickedness and whose soul is condemned to the cycle of rebirth,
entailing further suffering at lower levels of existence; whereas the

person who denies the will is like the holy man whose life of renunciation of sin is rewarded by release from rebirth with the attainment of nirvana. Thus, in volume II of *The World as Will and Representaion*, Schopenhauer maintains that 'as long as no denial of . . . will has taken place, that of us which is left over by death is the seed and kernel of quite another existence, in which a new individual finds himself again so fresh and original' (*WWR* II, p. 501). That is to say, a person's inner nature, the timeless act of will or force which constitutes his character, is unaffected by his death and may emerge at a later date in a new phenomenal individual who, with the same character, supplied through the father, and a new intellect, derived from the mother, will lead a new life of suffering with no memory of any previous existence.[24] In the light of this theory, the suicide's hope to escape suffering by choosing death is vain, for he cannot escape suffering in future lives. As well as failing to avoid future suffering, the suicide also misses the chance to achieve salvation. By renouncing willing a person's inner being eventually melts away, so that at death there is nothing remaining which can become the germ of a future new existence. 'For him who ends thus', says Schopenhauer, 'the world has at the same time ended' (*WWR* I, p. 382).

'I cannot stomach his hideous optimism', wrote one recent distinguished commentator on Schopenhauer's philosophy.[25] However, the term 'salvation' is misleading in that it misrepresents the bleakness of Schopenhauer's vision. His teaching, he says, 'ends with a negation' (*WWR* II, p. 612). That is to say, all that can be hoped for is not-living, non-existence. This is the nothingness which 'hovers behind all virtue and holiness' (*WWR* I, p. 411). It is this very negativity that is evaded by the mystical writers of all religious traditions, by, for instance, the Indian myths of reabsorption in Brahman and the nirvana of the Buddhists. Schopenhauer does not deny the beauty or the consolation to be found in the writings of the mystics but, unlike religion, philosophy is obliged to remain within the bounds of the knowable and the sayable. Schopenhauer is thus unable to say more than that, to those who have denied the will, 'the world . . . is nothing' (the first and last words of *The World as Will and Representation*).

For Schopenhauer, the world was never nothing. He never ceased to concern himself with the reception of his philosophy of renunciation. His wish, expressed in an autobiographical note of 1855, that the morning sun of his fame would gild the evening of his life and dispel its gloom (*MR* IV, p. 516), was realized. And he continued to revise his publications to ensure the continuation of his influence after his death. In the preface to the third edition of *The World as Will and Representation*, published once again by Brockhaus in September 1859, he based his hopes on the old rule that its influence would last the longer in proportion to the lateness of its beginning, and in the preface to the second edition of *The Two Fundamental Problems of Ethics*, published in August 1860, the last of his works he saw into print, he acknowledged that he had made a breakthrough with the learned public.

By this time, his health was failing. In April 1860 he had experienced palpitations and shortness of breath while returning home after dinner at the *Englischer Hof.* These symptoms persisted throughout the summer, forcing him to shorten his regular afternoon walks and to pause for breath. But he stubbornly refused to alter his daily regime and even to take the medicine his doctor prescribed. Early in September, Schopenhauer was seriously ill with an inflammation of the lungs and told his friend, the lawyer Wilhelmuon Gwinner, that he was dying, though he was soon well enough to leave his bed and receive visitors. A close friend since 1857, Gwinner became Schopenhauer's legal advisor after the death of Martin Emden in 1858, and was appointed executor of his will. Gwinner was the last of the friends to see Schopenhauer alive and described their final conversation in the biography he published soon after the philosopher's death.[26] They talked cheerfully of literature

Jules Lunteschütz, *Schopenhauer* (aged 71) *c.* 1859, oil on canvas.

and politics. Opening Isaac D'Israeli's *Curiosities of Literature* to the page about authors who had ruined their publishers, Schopenhauer remarked, jokingly, that he had nearly been driven to that. He also showed Gwinner a recent letter of appreciation he had received from some Austrian cadets and expressed his pleasure that his philosophy was now of value to a wide readership. He hoped to live long enough to make some revisions to his *Parerga und Paralipomena*, but while he had no fears of worms feeding on his corpse, he still felt anger at the mauling his spirit would receive from professors. When the maid brought in candles, Gwinner noticed that Schopenhauer's face showed no traces of illness. It would be a blessing, Schopenhauer remarked, for death to result in his total extinction but he had no prospect of that. Even so, he would die with a clear intellectual conscience (*G*, p. 396).

On the following day, 20 September, Schopenhauer experienced a violent spasm on rising from his bed, causing him to fall and injure his forehead. He slept well that night and took his customary cold bath and breakfast on the next morning. Maintaining the familiar routine, the maid opened the windows and left the room. A few minutes later the doctor arrived to find Schopenhauer leaning back in the corner of his sofa, dead. There were no signs of any 'violent transition'. No autopsy was performed and, in accordance with his wishes, Schopenhauer's body was left longer than normal in the mortuary to eliminate the possibility he feared of being buried alive. On a wet Wednesday, 26 September 1860, attended by a few friends, Schopenhauer's funeral service was taken by a Lutheran minister and the eulogy given by Gwinner. The simple gravestone of dark marble bore only the words 'Arthur Schopenhauer'.

8

'Posterity will erect monuments to me'

It was the Apostles and not the professors, as Schopenhauer had feared, who mauled his spirit in the immediate aftermath of his death. While preparing a new edition of *Parerga und Paralipomena* in 1861, Frauenstädt, the executor of Schopenhauer's writings, contacted Gwinner, the executor of Schopenhauer's will, about the manuscript (*About Myself*), containing autobiographical notes from 1821 onwards.[1] Gwinner had destroyed it in accordance, he claimed, with Schopenhauer's wishes, though he had made use of some passages in his biography of Schopenhauer which appeared in 1862. A squabble broke out amongst Schopenhauer's friends, some claiming that Schopenhauer had wanted the manuscript published and that Gwinner had plagiarized it. The dispute became public when Frauenstädt published his biography in 1863. Gwinner's defence was that Schopenhauer had already drawn on the manuscript in *Parerga und Paralipomena* and that what was lost were entirely personal remarks about himself and others which had no bearing on his philosophy. The publicity probably helped the friends in their task of promoting Schopenhauer's philosophy, and a major step was achieved when the first edition of Schopenhauer's collected works, edited by Frauenstädt, was published in 1873.

The divisions between the Schopenhauerians had nothing like the intensity and intellectual significance of the split between the Hegelians after the death of Hegel. Though lectures on Schopenhauer were given during his lifetime at various German universities, and even an essay competition held at Leipzig, there never was, and never would be, an academic school of Schopenhauerians. The absence of obscurity, strange words and ponderous sentences in Schopenhauer's writing meant that there was little scope for the philosophy professors to make a reputation by advancing some radical new interpretation of his philosophy. And, of the many distinguished university experts on Schopenhauer's philosophy, few, if any, would regard themselves as Schopenhauerians. His influence tends to be on thinkers who develop one or more of his dominant themes, such as his pessimism or irrationalism, in the course of fashioning a philosophy of their own – for example, Eduard von Hartmann in Germany and Henri Bergson in France in the second half of the nineteenth century, and Max Scheler in twentieth-century Germany.[2]

The greatest philosophers to have been influenced by Schopenhauer were Nietzsche and Wittgenstein, neither of whom enjoyed a conventional academic career, though both were for a time university professors. Both, too, encountered Schopenhauer in their youth and made use of his ideas in their early work but renounced them later. The extent of Schopenhauer's influence in their mature philosophies is a subject of endless fascination.

In 1865, as a twenty-one-year-old student in Leipzig, Nietzsche became enthralled by the philosophy of the 'gloomy genius' after buying a copy of *The World as Will and Representation* on impulse in a second-hand bookshop. He was befriended a few years later by another Schopenhauerian, Richard Wagner, with whose music Nietzsche was already enamoured. Through many intense discussions at Wagner's home at Tribschen, near Lucerne, Nietzsche was inspired to write his first book, *The Birth of Tragedy Out of the Spirit of Music* (1872), in which he drew on Schopenhauer's metaphysics to advocate the regeneration of European civilization through Wagnerian music drama. In doing so, however, he departed from Schopenhauer's view of art by proclaiming the life-affirming character of tragedy. The scandal created by the book's dubious classical scholarship and its association with the controversial figure of Wagner created difficulties for Nietzsche's position as Professor of Philology at Basel University, a post ill-health soon forced him to resign. At the same time that he began to distance himself from Wagner, his growing independence of mind made him more critical of Schopenhauer's view of the world. 'Schopenhauer . . . was wrong about everything', Nietzsche wrote in *Ecce Homo*,[3] his last book written shortly before his mental collapse in 1889. Though Nietzsche rejected most of Schopenhauer's views, their influence on his own philosophy is exhibited in numerous ways, not least by the importance he attached to the notion of the will to power, a concept arguably derived from Schopenhauer's notion of the will to life.

The notoriety of Wagner's operas and Nietzsche's philosophy towards the end of the nineteenth century contributed to the spread of interest in Schopenhauer. In *fin-de-siècle* Vienna, musicians such as Mahler and Schoenberg, artists such as Klimt and intellectuals such as Karl Kraus, Otto Weininger and Fritz Mauthner were avid readers of his work. Sigmund Freud paid tribute to Schopenhauer as a source for his own theories of the unconscious and of the role sex plays in the human psyche, though it is doubtful that Freud developed the theories through reading Schopenhauer. It was also in Vienna, early in the twentieth century, that the teenaged Ludwig Wittgenstein was introduced to Schopenhauer's *The World as Will and Representation* by his elder sister Gretl to help him come to terms with the loss of his faith. Schopenhauer's philosophy made a deep impression on him, yet it was problems in the foundations of mathematics and in logic, rather than Schopenhauer's philosophy, that led Wittgenstein, having trained as an engineer, to study philosophy under Bertrand Russell at Cambridge in 1911.

In the *Tractatus Logico-Philosophicus* (1921–2), Wittgenstein developed a view of the relation of language to the world that is not only radically un-Schopenhauerian but is antithetical to much of Schopenhauer's philosophy. Thus, on the picture theory of the proposition, idealism is nonsensical since it contravenes the limits of what can sensibly be said. Yet the *Tractatus*, as well as the notebooks that Wittgenstein kept during the first World War, contain numerous remarks that are indubitably Schopenhauerian in tone: for example, the proposition that the metaphysical subject is not a part but a limit of the world, as well as the remarks on ethics – 'The only life that is happy is the life that can renounce the amenities of the world' – and aesthetics – 'The work of art is the object seen *sub specie aeternitatis*'.[4] Given the anti-theoretical character of Wittgenstein's thought at the time of writing the *Tractatus*, it is difficult to take these Schopenhauerian-sounding remarks at face value as expressions of philosophical doctrines in the sense that Schopenhauer understood them. The issue here is more fraught with respect to the later philosophy of Wittgenstein which emerged in the 1930s and '40s. There he explicitly asserts that he wants to do away with all philosophical theories.[5] Nevertheless, it has been argued that what Wittgenstein has to say about language and meaning in the *Philosophical Investigations* commits him to some form of transcendental idealism, though, if this is true, it could be explained as an expression of what he absorbed from Kant rather than specifically from Schopenhauer.

As in his life, so after his death, it was the non-academics who were most enthusiastic in their response to Schopenhauer – the educated public and, in particular, creative writers. Tolstoy, Turgenev, Zola, Maupassant, Proust, Thomas Mann, Kafka, Melville, Hardy, Conrad, Shaw and D. H. Lawrence were all admirers of Schopenhauer's philosophy: some, such as Lawrence, were later to reject it, while for others, such as Mann, it was an influence which deepened throughout the course of their lives.[6] What attracted these great writers to Schopenhauer was not his treatment of Kantian transcendental idealism but rather the view of life and the world presented with a compelling vividness worthy of a literary artist. While Mann compared *The World as Will and Representation* to a great symphony in four movements, it might with more justice be thought of as a narrative of the origin, life and death of the human individual. Schopenhauer continued to influence creative artists in the twentieth century – Samuel Beckett and Jorge Luis Borges are the most prominent – though to nothing like the same extent as in the nineteenth. For the writers reared at the end of the nineteenth century, Schopenhauer was an ally in their struggle against the prevailing ethos of confidence and hope in the future of mankind. The shattering of that confidence due to the horrors perpetrated in the course of the twentieth century, reinforced by the artists who had absorbed his teaching, meant that the grim truth about existence that Schopenhauer had presented with ruthless honesty could at last be acknowledged.

Friedrich Schierholz, bronze memorial bust of Schopenhauer, 1890s, in
Wallanlagen Park, Frankfurt am Main.

References

Introduction

1 Anton Chekhov, *Uncle Vanya*, trans. Ronald Hingley, *Five Plays* (Oxford, 1980), Act III, p. 155.
2 Simone Weil, quoted by Jacques Cabaud, *Simone Weil: A Fellowship in Love* (London, 1964), Introduction.
3 David E. Cartwright, *Schopenhauer: A Biography* (Cambridge, 2010); Rüdiger Safranski, *Schopenhauer and the Wild Years of Philosophy*, trans. Ewald Osers (London, 1989); Arthur Hübscher, *The Philosophy of Schopenhauer in its Intellectual Context*, trans. Joachim T. Bare and David E. Cartwright (Lewiston, Lampeter and Queenston, 1987).
4 W. Wallace, *Life of Arthur Schopenhauer* (London, 1890).
5 *The Cambridge Edition of the Works of Schopenhauer*, ed. Christopher Janaway (Cambridge, 2009).

1 The Sins of the Father

1 Johanna Schopenhauer, *My Youthful Life* (London, 1847), vol. II, p. 103.
2 Helen Zimmern, *Arthur Schopenhauer: His Life and his Philosophy* (Gloucester, 2008), p. 4.
3 Patrick Bridgwater, *Arthur Schopenhauer's English Schooling* (London, 1988), p. 11.
4 W. Wallace, *Life of Arthur Schopenhauer* (London, 1890), p. 22.
5 Joanna Schopenhauer, *My Youthful Life*, p. 24.
6 Ibid., p. 108.
7 See Bridgwater, *Arthur Schopenhauer's English Schooling*, pp. 16–18.

8 From 1821 Schopenhauer made occasional notes about his life, together with general reflections, under the title Εἰς ἑαυτόν (*About Myself*). Although the original was destroyed after his death, a reconstruction of the manuscript is provided by Arthur Hübscher in *MR* IV, pp. 483–520.

9 This remark comes from the *curriculum vitae* that Schopenhauer submitted to the University of Berlin in 1819 in support of his application for a lectureship there. The original Latin, and a German translation, are provided in *GB*, pp. 47–55 and 647–56 (649).

10 See Rüdiger Safranski, *Schopenhauer and the Wild Years of Philosophy*, trans. Ewald Osers (London, 1989), pp. 28–9.

11 Bridgwater, *Arthur Schopenhauer's English Schooling*, p. 284.

12 David E. Cartwright, *Schopenhauer, A Biography* (Cambridge, 2010), p. 29. See also Arthur Hübscher, *The Philosophy of Schopenhauer in its Intellectual Context*, trans. Joachim T. Bare and David E. Cartwright (Lewiston, Lampeter, Queenston, 1987), p. 3; and Bridgwater, *Arthur Schopenhauer's English Schooling*, p. 283.

13 See Safranski, *Schopenhauer and the Wild Years of Philosophy*, pp. 32–3.

14 In a letter to her son written from Weimar in 1807, Johanna claimed that it was her plan for Arthur to go into the Church as a step towards university, a plan which, she alleged, Heinrich cruelly thwarted. See Ludger Lütkehaus, ed., *Die Schopenhauers: Der Familien-Briefwechsel* (Munich, 1991), pp. 164 and 168–9.

15 In 1813–14, when she was establishing her literary career, Johanna published the diary she kept of her travels in England and Scotland. The second edition of 1818 was translated into English in 1988. See Johanna Schopenhauer, *A Lady Travels: The Diaries of Johanna Schopenhauer*, trans. Ruth Michaelis-Jena and Willy Merson (London, 1988). Arthur was required by his parents to keep his own diary so that he could practise his handwriting, a matter to which Heinrich attached great importance owing to the need for a businessman to write in a clear and firm hand. See Arthur Schopenhauer, *Reisetagebücher aus den Jahren 1803–4*, ed. Charlotte von Gwinner (Leipzig, 1923). Bridgwater provides a translation of the English section of the diary, together with extensive notes, in chapter 3 of *Arthur Schopenhauer's English Schooling*, pp. 97–139.

16 Johanna may have been mistaken when she claimed in her diary that two of Nelson's nephews had been educated at Revd Lancaster's

school. Nonetheless, Nelson and Lady Hamilton were regular members of Revd Lancaster's congregation in Merton, where he was acting curate, from 1801–03, and they were guests in one another's homes. Later, Lancaster's eldest son, Henry, served under Nelson on the *Victory* at the Battle of Trafalgar.

17 This and subsequent quotations from the letters to Arthur are taken from Bridgwater, *Arthur Schopenhauer's English Schooling*, pp. 236ff.

18 Johanna, too, found British sabbatarianism difficult to get along with, as she made clear at some length in her account of her travels in northern Britain. See Johanna Schopenhauer, *A Lady Travels*, p. 162f.

19 See Safranski, *Schopenhauer and the Wild Years of Philosophy*, p. 49.

20 See ibid., pp. 50–51.

21 Lütkehaus, ed., *Die Schopenhauers*, pp. 64–6.

22 Bridgwater, *Arthur Schopenhauer's English Schooling*, pp. 237, 250.

23 Lütkehaus, ed., *Die Schopenhauers*, p. 74.

24 *An die Musik*, a poem by Franz von Schober and set to music by Schubert in 1817. Translation in Richard Wigmore, trans., *Schubert: The Complete Song Texts* (London, 1992), p. 44.

25 Wilhelm Heinrich Wackenroder, 'The Marvels of the Musical Art', published in a collection of essays edited by Ludwig Tieck under the title *Phantasien über die Kunst, für Freunde der Kunst* (1799). Arthur, like Jean Paul and others, mistakenly took Tieck to be the author of the essay. The essay is translated by Mary Hurst Schubert in her edition of Wackenroder's essays, *Confessions and Fantasies* (University Park and London, 1971), pp. 178–81.

26 See Hübscher, *The Philosophy of Schopenhauer in its Intellectual Context*, p. 38.

27 This point is made by Safranski, *Schopenhauer and the Wild Years of Philosophy*, p. 56.

28 Lütkehaus, ed., *Die Schopenhauers*, p. 166.

2 A High Mountain Road

1 See Ludger Lütkehaus, ed., *Die Schopenhauers, Der Familien-Briefwechsel* (Munich, 1991), p. 199.

2 See ibid., p. 200.

3 Quotations taken from Johanna Schopenhauer, *My Youthful Life* (London, 1847), vol. II, pp. 263ff. For Johanna's letters, see Lütkehaus, ed., *Die Schopenhauers*, pp. 80–103.

4 Lütkehaus, ed., *Die Schopenhauers*, p. 108.

5 Passow's *Dictionary of the Greek Language* (4th edn 1831), compiled when he was Professor at the University of Breslau, became the basis of Liddell and Scott's Greek–English Lexicon.

6 Arthur Schopenhauer, *Manuscript Remains*, ed. Arthur Hübscher, trans. E.F.J. Payne (Oxford, 1974), vols I–IV.

7 Arthur Hübscher, *The Philosophy of Schopenhauer in its Intellectual Context*, trans. Joachim T. Bare and David E. Cartwright (Lewiston, Lampeter and Queenston, 1987), p. 10.

8 Johanna's memoir of Fernow's life, published in 1810, was the first of her many publications.

9 David E. Cartwright, *Schopenhauer: A Biography* (Cambridge, 2010), p. 136.

10 See Rüdiger Safranski, *Schopenhauer and the Wild Years of Philosophy*, trans. Ewald Osers (London, 1989), p. 102.

3 Dr Schopenhauer

1 Quotation taken from Rüdiger Safranski, *Schopenhauer and the Wild Years of Philosophy,* trans. Ewald Osers (London, 1989), p. 147.

2 Schopenhauer had visited Pestalozzi's school in Switzerland while on his European tour with his parents in 1804. See David E. Cartwright, *Schopenhauer: A Biography* (Cambridge, 2010), pp. 81–3.

3 See Nicholas Boyle, *German Literature: A Very Short Introduction* (Oxford, 2008), p. 73.

4 H. Zimmern, *Arthur Schopenhauer: His Life and Work* (Gloucester, 2008), p. 24. Schopenhauer also visited the charity hospital in Berlin to study the treatment given to diseases of the mind as well as of the body.

5 However, of all the lecturers he kept in touch with, it was the classicist Friedrich August Wolf whom he held in the greatest esteem. See *MR* IV, p. 501.

6 D. Cartwright, 'Introduction' to *WN*, p. xvii.

7 I. Kant, *Critique of Pure Reason*, trans. Norman Kemp Smith (London, 1964), Bxvi, p. 22.

8 Ibid., Bxx, p. 24.

9 J. Fichte, *Wissenschaftslehre, Sämtliche Werke* (Leipzig, 1834–46), vol. I, pp. 425ff; quoted by C. Janaway, *Self and World in Schopenhauer's Philosophy* (Oxford, 1989), p. 83.

10 See the translation of the original edition of *The Fourfold Root of the Principle of Sufficient Reason* in F. C. White, *Schopenhauer's Early Fourfold Root* (Aldershot, 1997), p. 68.

11 Schopenhauer adopts the version of the principle formulated in Latin by the German, pre-Kantian, rationalist philosopher Christian Wolff (1679–1754), *Nihil est sine ratione cur potius sit quam non sit*.

4 The Great Work

1 Ludger Lütkehaus, ed., *Die Schopenhauers, Der Familien-Briefwechsel* (Munich, 1991), p. 214.

2 Further details of Adele's life can be found in Gabrielle Büch, *Alles Leben ist Traum: Adele Schopenhauer, eine Biographie* (Berlin, 2002).

3 Lütkehaus, ed., *Die Schopenhauers*, pp. 220–22. English translation taken from Rüdiger Safranski, *Schopenhauer and the Wild Years of Philosophy*, trans. Ewald Osers (London, 1989), p. 170.

4 To Schopenhauer's disappointment, Gans returned to Berlin.

5 Other recipients included Herr Kabrun, the Danzig merchant to whom Schopenhauer had been first apprenticed; Gottlob Schulze at Göttingen, his first philosophy teacher; and Professors Wolf and Schleiermacher at Berlin.

6 Quotation taken from David E. Cartwright, *Schopenhauer: A Biography* (Cambridge, 2010), p. 243.

7 They never have been proved; and they cannot be, for Schopenhauer's physiological speculation is not specific enough to be capable of either confirmation or refutation.

8 J. W. von Goethe, 'Lähmung', in *Goethes Gedichte*; quoted by Schopenhauer in *On Vision and Colors*, trans. E.F.J. Payne (Oxford, 1994), p. 8.

9 Safranski, *Schopenhauer and the Wild Years of Philosophy*, p. 195.

Friedrich Kind was the librettist for Weber's opera *Der Freischütz* (1821), the plot of which was based on a ghost story written by Friedrich Laun and August Apel.

10 Quoted by Cartwright, *Schopenhauer*, pp. 281–2.

11 Abraham Hyacinthe Anquetil-Duperron, *Oupnek'hat (id est, secretum tegendum)*, (Paris, 1801–2), 2 vols.

12 Kant had – mistakenly, according to Schopenhauer – tried to distinguish his own Transcendental Idealism from Berkeley's Empirical Idealism, especially in the second edition of his *Critique of Pure Reason* (1787), the only edition available to Schopenhauer at this time. For a penetrating discussion of Schopenhauer's idealism in relation to Kant's, see Christopher Janaway, *Self and World in Schopenhauer's Philosophy* (Oxford, 1989), chapter 5.

13 Schopenhauer addresses this issue in the second edition of *The World as Will and Representation*. See chapter Seven below.

14 See Bryan Magee, *The Philosophy of Schopenhauer*, revd edn (Oxford and New York, 1997), p. 144.

15 A point made by Frederick Copleston, *A History of Philosophy*, vol. VII: *Fichte to Nietzsche* (London and New York, 1963), p. 287.

5 The Art of Genius

1 Ludger Lütkehaus, ed., *Die Schopenhauers, Der Familien-Briefwechsel* (Munich, 1991), pp. 294–5. Schopenhauer fathered another illegitimate daughter in 1835–6 in Frankfurt, as he reported to his friend Anthime Grégoire in December 1836 (*GB*, p. 158). This child also soon died.

2 Schopenhauer returned a copy of Hegel's *Logic* to the owner in November 1813, apparently unread (*GB* p. 6). He borrowed it again for a few days in September 1818, after he had completed the manuscript of *The World as Will and Representation*. See Arthur Hübscher, *The Philosophy of Schopenhauer in its Intellectual Context*, trans. Joachim T. Bare and David E. Cartwright (Lewiston, Lampeter and Queenston, 1987), p. 276.

3 See David E. Cartwright, *Schopenhauer: A Biography* (Cambridge, 2010), pp. 363–4, for an account of the *viva voce*.

4 *Privatdozent* literally means private lecturer. Although it was an

unsalaried post, payment was obtained for delivering lectures.

5 See Cartwright, *Schopenhauer*, pp. 380–93 for a detailed assessment of the reviews of *The World as Will and Representation*.

6 Friedrich Nietzsche, *Ecce Homo*, trans. Duncan Large (Oxford, 2009), foreword, section 3, p. 4.

7 Immanuel Kant, *Critique of the Power of Judgment*, trans. Paul Guyer and Eric Matthews (Cambridge, 2000).

8 Kant, 'First Moment of the Judgment of Taste', ibid., §§1–5, pp. 89–96.

9 T. S. Eliot, 'The Dry Salvages', *Four Quartets* (London, 1943), v, ll. 210–12.

10 Payne's translation of Spinoza's Latin quoted by Schopenhauer. See Spinoza, *Ethics*, v, prop. 31, schol ivm.

11 William Wordsworth, 'Lines Composed A Few Miles Above Tintern Abbey', first published in *Lyrical Ballads* (Bristol, 1798), l. 59.

12 For Kant's account of the Sublime, see Kant, *Critique of the Power of Judgment*, §§23–9, pp. 128–58. Schopenhauer judged Kant's theory of the Sublime superior to his theory of the beautiful (*WWR* I, p. 532).

13 Hübscher, *The Philosophy of Schopenhauer in its Intellectual Context*, p. 27. See also Cartwright, *Schopenhauer*, p. 116 and n. 73.

14 For a discussion of Schopenhauer's theory of laughter, see Peter B. Lewis, 'Schopenhauer's Laughter', *The Monist*, LXXXVIII/1 (January 2005), pp. 36–51.

6 The Mystery of Compassion

1 The sample contains Schopenhauer's preferred translations of some terms crucial both to Kant's and his own philosophy: 'perception' for *Anschauung* and 'idea' for *Vorstellung*. See David E. Cartwright, *Schopenhauer: A Biography* (Cambridge, 2010), p. 372, n. 97.

2 The company was now in the hands of the sons of Friedrich Arnold Brockhaus, the publisher of the first edition of *The World as Will and Representation*, who had died in August 1823.

3 The agent who had managed their common property at Ohra in the vicinity of Danzig had died, leaving his accounts in the red.

4 Ludger Lütkehaus, ed., *Die Schopenhauers, Der Familien-Briefwechsel* (Munich, 1991), p. 337.

5 In the Appendix to the essay, coyly omitted from the first English

translation of *The World as Will and Representation* (1883), Schopenhauer accounts for male homosexual relationships as a way of preventing men from fathering inferior offspring which would weaken the species (*WWR* II, p. 565).

6 Cartwright, *Schopenhauer*, p. 428. See ibid., pp. 423–9 for a detailed account of Schopenhauer's correspondence with Rosenkranz and Schubert.

7 See Julian Young, *Schopenhauer* (London and New York, 2005), pp. 82–7 for more detail on this issue. Young argues that Schopenhauer's view of the Will as a blind force is in conflict with his teleological explanation of adaptation.

8 The memoirs were edited and published by Adele in 1839. They were translated into English under the title *Youthful Life and Pictures of Travel: Being the Autobiography of Madame Schopenhauer* (London, 1847).

9 Christopher Janaway points out that Schopenhauer wrote on his copy of *The Two Fundamental Problems of Ethics* that 'the real judge of the essay in Copenhagen had been a Hegelian academic, called Martensen, author of a Hegelian theory of morals and later a bishop', (Christopher Janaway, 'Introduction', *The Two Fundamental Problems of Ethics* (Cambridge, 2009), p. xxxix). In the circumstances, the surprise would have been greater if Schopenhauer *had* been awarded the prize.

10 T. S. Eliot, 'Little Gidding', *Four Quartets*, section II, l. 88.

7 The Sage of Frankfurt

1 See Arthur Hübscher, *The Philosophy of Schopenhauer in its Intellectual Context*, trans. Joachim T. Bare and David E. Cartwright (Lewiston, Lampeter and Queenston, 1987), p. 508, n. 17.

2 Quoted by John E. Atwell, *Schopenhauer on the Character of the World: The Metaphysics of the World* (Berkeley, Los Angeles and London, 1995), p. 113.

3 Christopher Janaway provides a useful overview of the competing interpretations in part VI of his essay 'Will and Nature', in *The Cambridge Companion to Schopenhauer*, ed. Christopher Janaway (Cambridge, 1999), pp. 158–65.

4 Theognis, *Fragments* 425, quoted by Schopenhauer in *The World as Will and Representation*, trans. E.F.J. Payne (New York, 1969), II, p. 586.

5 Quoted by Rüdiger Safranski, *Schopenhauer and the Wild Years of Philosophy,* trans. Ewald Osers (London, 1989), p. 324.

6 See Ludger Lütkehaus, ed., *Die Schopenhauers: Der Familien-Briefwechsel* (Munich, 1991), pp. 490–91.

7 Ibid., p. 491.

8 Ibid., pp. 458–9.

9 *The Westminster Review*, vol. LIX (April 1853), pp. 388–407.

10 Ibid., p. 394.

11 For further details, see Hübscher, *The Philosophy of Schopenhauer in its Intellectual Context*, pp. 363–4.

12 It was Dorguth, the 'primary evangelist', who had likened Schopenhauer to Casper Hauser, a teenaged boy who appeared on the streets of Nuremberg in 1828 claiming to have grown up isolated in a darkened cell. The mystery of Hauser's origins and his alleged links to the royal house of Baden, as well as his violent death in 1833, were the source of much intellectual debate and popular scandal.

13 Nicholas Boyle, *German Literature: A Very Short Introduction* (Oxford, 2008), p. 81.

14 Friedrich Engels, *Anti-Düring* (1878) in K. Marx and F. Engels, *Selected Works* (Moscow, 1970), vol. III, pp. 61–2.

15 Richard Wagner, letter to Franz Liszt, December 1854, in *Selected Letters of Richard Wagner*, trans. and ed. Stewart Spencer and Barry Millington (London and Melbourne, 1987), p. 323.

16 Richard Wagner, letter to August Röckel, 23 August 1856, ibid., p. 357.

17 Richard Wagner, *My Life* (Cambridge, 1983), pp. 508–10.

18 For further detail, see Ernest Newman, *The Life of Richard Wagner* (Cambridge, 1976), vol. II, and Bryan Magee, *Wagner and Philosophy* (London, 2001).

19 Quoted by Hübscher, *The Philosophy of Schopenhauer in its Intellectual Context*, p. 428.

20 Quotations from Newman, *The Life of Richard Wagner*, pp. 432–3.

21 Quoted by Helen Zimmern, *Arthur Schopenhauer: His Life and His Philosophy* (Gloucester, 2008), p. 152.

22 Shakespeare, *Measure For Measure*, III, i, ll. 132–5.

23 Diogenes Laërtius, quoted by Schopenhauer, *WWR* II, p. 468.

24 Schopenhauer distinguishes this process of palingenesis, requiring the decomposition and reconstruction of individuals, from metempsy-

chosis, which involves the transmission of a complete soul from one individual life to another (*WWR* II, pp. 502f; see also *PP* II, pp. 276f).

25 A. Phillips Griffiths, 'Wittgenstein and the Four-Fold Root', *Proceedings of the Aristotelian Society*, suppl. vol. L (1976), p. 3.

26 W. Gwinner, *Arthur Schopenhauer aus persönlichen Umgange dargestellt . . .* (Leipzig, 1922), pp. 195–204.

8 'Posterity will erect monuments to me'

The epigraph to this chapter is taken from Arthur Schopenhauer, *Manuscript Remains*, ed. Arthur Hübscher, trans. E.F.J. Payne (Oxford, 1988) vol III, p. 11. Original manuscript version written in Rome, April 1819.

1 A reconstruction of the manuscript, together with an account of its history, is provided by Arthur Hübscher in *MR* IV, pp. 472–520.

2 For an account of Hartmann's and Bergson's philosophies in relation to Schopenhauer, see Frederick Copleston, *Arthur Schopenhauer: Philosopher of Pessimism* (London, 1975), chap. 10, pp. 190–212. On Scheler's relation to Schopenhauer, see Arthur Hübscher, *The Philosophy of Schopenhauer in Its Intellectual Context*, trans. Joachim T. Bare and David E. Cartwright (Lewiston, Lampeter and Queenston, 1987), pp. 395–6.

3 Friedrich Nietzsche, *Ecce Homo*, trans. Duncan Large (Oxford, 2007), 'The Birth of Tragedy', p. 45.

4 Ludwig Wittgenstein, *Tractatus Logico-Philosophicus*, trans. D. Pears and B. McGuinness (London, 1961), 5.641; Ludwig Wittgenstein, *Notebooks, 1914–1916*, trans. G.E.M. Anscombe (Oxford, 1979), pp. 81, 83.

5 Ludwig Wittgenstein, *Philosophical Investigations*, trans. G.E.M. Anscombe, revd 4th edn, P.M.S. Hacker and Joachim Schulte (Chichester, 2009), §109.

6 See Bryan Magee, *The Philosophy of Schopenhauer*, revd edn (Oxford and New York, 1997), chap. 18, and Robert L. Wicks, *Schopenhauer's The World as Will and Representation* (London and New York, 2011), chap. 4, for details of the influence of Schopenhauer on creative artists.

Bibliography

For Schopenhauer's works, see Abbreviations on page 7.

Secondary Literature

Atwell, John E., *Schopenhauer on the Character of the World: The Metaphysics of Will* (Berkeley, Los Angeles, London, 1995)

Boyle, Nicholas, *German Literature: A Very Short Introduction* (Oxford, 2008)

Bridgwater, Patrick, *Arthur Schopenhauer's English Schooling* (London, 1988)

Büch, Gabrielle, *Alle Leben ist Traum: Adele Schopenhauer, eine Biographie* (Berlin, 2002)

Cartwright, David E., *Historical Dictionary of Schopenhauer's Philosophy* (Lanham, MD, 2005)

——, *Schopenhauer: A Biography* (Cambridge, 2010)

Copleston, Frederick, *Arthur Schopenhauer: Philosopher of Pessimism* (London, 1975)

——, *A History of Philosophy*, vol. VII: *Fichte to Nietzsche* (London and New York, 1963)

Engels, Friedrich, *Anti-Düring* [1878], in K. Marx and F. Engels, *Selected Works* (Moscow, 1970), vol. III

Fichte, J., *Wissenschaftslehre, Sämtliche Werke*, ed. J. H. Fichte (Leipzig, 1834–46)

Gardiner, Patrick, *Schopenhauer* (Harmondsworth, 1963)

Griffiths, A. Phillips, 'Wittgenstein and the Four-fold Root', *Proceedings of the Aristotelian Society*, suppl. vol. L (1976)

Hübscher, Arthur, *The Philosophy of Schopenhauer in its Intellectual Context*, trans. Joachim T. Baer and David E. Cartwright (Lewiston, Lampeter and Queenston, 1989)

Janaway, Christopher, ed., *The Cambridge Companion to Schopenhauer* (Cambridge, 1999)

——, ed., *The Cambridge Edition of the Works of Schopenhauer* (Cambridge, 2009)

——, *Schopenhauer: A Very Short Introduction* (Oxford, 2002)

——, *Self and World in Schopenhauer's Philosophy* (Oxford, 1989)

Lewis, Peter B., 'Schopenhauer's Laughter', *The Monist*, LXXXVIII/1 (January 2005), pp. 36–51

——, 'Schopenhauer's Aesthetics', in *Key Writers on Art: From Antiquity to the Nineteenth Century*, ed. Charles Murray (London, 2002), pp. 167–72

Kant, I., *Critique of Pure Reason*, trans. Norman Kemp Smith (London, 1964)

——, *Critique of the Power of Judgment*, trans. Paul Guyer and Eric Matthews (Cambridge, 2000)

Lütkehaus, Ludger, ed., *Die Schopenhauers: Der Familien-Briefwechsel von Adele, Arthur, Heinrich Floris und Johanna Schopenhauer* (Munich, 1998)

Magee, Bryan, *The Philosophy of Schopenhauer*, revd edn (Oxford, 1997)

——, *Wagner and Philosophy* (London, 2001)

Mann, Thomas, 'Schopenhauer' [1938], in *Essays of Three Decades*, trans. H. T. Lowe-Porter (New York, 1947), pp. 372–410

Newman, Ernest, *The Life of Richard Wagner* (Cambridge, 1976), 4 vols

Nietzsche, Friedrich, *Ecce Homo*, trans. Duncan Large (Oxford, 2009)

Oxenford, John, *The Westminster Review*, LIX (April 1853), pp. 388–407

Safranski, Rüdiger, *Schopenhauer and the Wild Years of Philosophy*, trans. Ewald Osers (London, 1989)

Schopenhauer, Johanna, *A Lady Travels: The Diaries of Johanna Schopenhauer*, trans. Ruth Michaelis-Jena and Willy Merson (London, 1988)

——, *My Youthful Life* (London, 1847), vols I–II

Stern, Carola, *'Alles, was ich in der Welt verlange': Das Leben der Johanna Schopenhauer* (Hamburg, 2005)

Tanner, Michael, *Schopenhauer* (London, 1997)

Wagner, Richard, *My Life* (Cambridge, 1983)

——, *Selected Letters of Richard Wagner*, trans. and ed. Stewart Spencer and Barry Millington (London and Melbourne, 1987)

Wallace, W., *Life of Arthur Schopenhauer* (London, 1890)

Wackenroder, Wilhelm Heinrich, 'The Marvels of the Musical Art', trans. Mary Hurst Schubert, in *Confessions and Fantasies* (University Park, PA, and London, 1971), pp. 178–81

Wicks, Robert L., *Schopenhauer's The World as Will and Representation* (London and New York, 2011)

Wittgenstein, Ludwig, *Notebooks 1914–1916*, trans. G.E.M. Anscombe (Oxford, 1979)

——, *Philosophical Investigations*, trans. G.E.M. Anscombe, revised 4th edn by P.M.S. Hacker and Joachim Schulte (Chichester, 2009)

——, *Tractatus Logico-Philosophicus*, trans. D. Pears and B. McGuinness (London, 1961)

Young, Julian, *Schopenhauer* (London and New York, 2005)

——, *Willing and Unwilling: A Study in the Philosophy of Arthur Schopenhauer* (Dordrecht, 1987)

Zimmer, Robert, *Arthur Schopenhauer, Ein philosophischer Weltbürger* (Munich, 2010)

Zimmern, H., *Arthur Schopenhauer: His Life and Work* [1876] (Gloucester, 2008)

Acknowledgements

I should like to thank two anonymous readers of the manuscript for their comments and suggestions. I am very grateful to Mr Stephen Roeper of the Goethe University of Frankfurt am Main for kindly showing me the Library's Schopenhauer-Archive and for his generous help. Friends from both sides of the Border have provided much needed encouragement over many years. My greatest debt is to my wife, Dorothy, whose love and support have sustained me throughout.